In Switzerland The Moon Is Always Male

Paul Gilk

Cover photo: Metal artwork on stucco wall of
DLZ in Winterthur, CH. Artist unknown.

Photos in text by Paul Gilk and Susanna Juon-Gilk.
Back cover photo by Irma Schoch-Juon.

First Edition

ISBN: 0-9675785-0-7

Library of Congress: 99-091703

Published by
Paul Gilk
The Log House
N3920 County E
Merrill, WI 54452

Printed in the United States of America by
Palmer Publications, Inc.
318 N. Main Street
Amherst, WI 54406

Acknowledgments

There are many people who, in some way or other, made our trip
to Switzerland possible. Some of these remain anonymous and
behind the scenes—the woman who sold us the tickets,
the airplane pilots, the people who handle baggage—and there are
many whose helpfulness is described in the pages that follow.
I thank them one and all.

But there are four people who must be named: Rhonda Brand,
Andreas Juon, Irma Schoch-Juon, and Annemarie Frick.
These four not only made our trip possible,
they—well, read on....

Prologue

Oh! the sorrow, *das Leid*, of correcting errors! *Das Leid*: in German, sorrow has no gender!

It's impossible to know, this rainy day in May, just what form this much-corrected manuscript will eventually assume. At the moment, it's a blotchy typescript (*ein beflecktes Manuskript*), having smeared upon it approximately two quarts of "Wite Out" and several pints of ballpoint ink. My typewriter keys are coated with white correcting fluid. There are fragments of my beard (the former *Rotbart*) scattered all over the log house.

Not only am I swearing off German in any form, tense, gender or would-be gender, I am seriously considering taking up English as a Second Language or maybe signing up for a correspondence course in Illiteracy.

Oh! dear reader, if you only knew what *Plage*, travail, has been borne in *dem Gekritzel*, the scribbling, of this *grammatikalische Katastrophe*! And the worst of it all is this: in German, sorrow has no gender! What indignity! What sardonic humor!

But what a blessing to have a Swiss wife who knows her articles and tenses, who is far more than a particular inflection form of a verb expressing a specific time distinction, tautly tense—past, present, and future perfect—*mein Omali*.

But even with an inhouse expert, so to speak, there are difficult questions: does one spell Romansh (that quaint one percent language of Graubunden) as Romansh or Romansch? For that matter, does one say "Graubunden"—this is the southeasterly canton in which the Viamala waits for its daily prey of tourists—or does one spell the word Graubünden, as they say in *Schweizerdeutsch*, or, as I've also seen, "*Schwyzerdütsch*," with the two little dots over the vowel, called *Umlaut* ("om-lout") or "vowel mutation"? Or (we're still on the question of Graubunden) does one say "Grigioni" (the Italian way) or "Grischun" (the Romansh way) or "Grisons" (the French way)?

Not only does Swiss German deviate from *Hochdeutsch*, High German, Switzerland also has French, Italian, and Romansh as official languages. These language/population groups are to some extent distinct regions: French in the west (twenty percent), Italian in the south (ten percent). Add to this Romansh scattered in the valleys of Graubünden and Ticino. The rest are German speakers—*Sprecherin* if female, *Sprecher* if male.

So how about imposing some neutral words—like our use of the term "chairperson," for instance? Well, "chair" in German is *Stuhl*, and *Stuhl* is male. And a stool pigeon? Sorry, a pigeon is *Taube* and *Taube* is female. If you are one of those persons who wishes to rip the sex out of speech, stamp the gender out of language, I recommend a little vacation in *der Schweiz*.

And if you're not yet totally *verwirrt*, bewildered, you might as well know that the name Switzerland derives from one of the three "forest cantons" (Uri, Schwyz, Unterwalden) that formed the original confederation in the year 1291. (Uri is the legendary home of Wilhelm Tell who shot the apple off his son's head with an arrow.) These were, and still are, German-speaking areas.

But there is an oval white sticker on the rear ends of many Swiss cars. In this white oval are the black letters CH. Now what does CH have to do with Switzerland? It is the Confederation Helvetia.

The Helvetians, or Helvetii, were a tribe of people who lived in what's now Switzerland. In 58 B.C., they decided to leave in a mass migration to the west, to what's now France. Caesar got wind of this, rushed from Rome, defeated them in battle, and forced them to return.

So Switzerland is the Confederation Helvetia because Julius Caesar interrupted the mass exodus of the Helvetii nearly sixty years before Jesus was born. Now there are roosters on the steeples of some Swiss churches....

And, if you think Swiss roosters say cock-a-doo-dle-doo, you've got another crow, *chreie* ("cry-a"), coming. *Kick-er-i-ki!*

Introduction

All things have a beginning, even if that beginning is somewhat arbitrary. This story begins on July 22, 1995.

It was a late Saturday afternoon, hot. Susanna and I were tired: not only had we hosted a group of travelling Mennonites at our century-old, hand-hewn and reconstructed log house the previous evening, we had also, all day Saturday, been the musical entertainment—Susanna on the violin she'd made herself, over twenty-five years ago, in Switzerland, and I on my Mexican guitar—at an art-and-craft fair in northern Wisconsin, near the Michigan border.

By prior arrangement, we stopped on our way home at the house of Susanna's former husband, near Eagle River, and we met with Susanna's oldest daughter, Rhonda, who was up from Chicago with her Pakistani husband, Imtiaz. The men were gone fishing and Rhonda had bad news: Susanna's oldest sister, Julia ("Yulia"), the opera singer, had called from Germany to say Mama was sick, weak, couldn't or wouldn't get up.

That night Susanna called Julia. The next day she called Frau Doktor Annemarie Frick, in Switzerland, a close friend of the Juon family. The sense of urgency was lessened by this latter call, in particular. We decided not to cancel our remaining musical engagements.

Later in the week, Susanna's father, Andreas, called from home in Switzerland to say Mama was in a local hospital, and not to worry. Things were under control. Susanna relaxed, a little. But we both realized Susanna would go to Switzerland in the near future. I began to think that maybe Woody, my eight year-old son, and I might come along.

Toward the end of August, Susanna and I (both of us pushing fifty) decided on September 22, a Friday, as our wedding day. Woody returned from northern Minnesota, near Lake Superior and the Canadian border, after spending the summer with his mom. We were busy, we were well, but we were always a little nervous about Mama.

On September 18, Susanna and Woody and I moved into the log

house for keeps. Our friend Charlie Green came to help, but he showed up with a face so swollen by an abscessed tooth that his nose was crooked. Susanna took one look at Charlie and drove him to our dentist friend, Mark Mehlos.

And, on September 22, an unseasonably cold day with snow in the air, Susanna and I were married in the United Methodist Church, in Merrill. We played and sang Psalm 100, as written and arranged by Susanna's father. We were married by two pastors, just to be sure.

In late October, the wild geese and red-gold leaves long gone, and more frequent snow flurries blustering about, Susanna proposed we go to Switzerland, for a month or six weeks, in late winter or early spring. In mid-November, we reluctantly told Woody we'd decided not to take him with us this time, because of the anticipated stresses. He cried.

On Thursday morning, November 30, I applied for a passport at the Tomahawk post office. The fee was $65. The woman who helped said I'd have a passport in my hands, through the mail, in three weeks, four at the most. Susanna and I planned to leave for Switzerland in early January.

In mid-December, Susanna bought us round-trip airline tickets, nontransferable and nonrefundable. We were scheduled to leave from Central Wisconsin Airport, in Mosinee, on January 11, 1996. On Christmas Day I wrote in my journal: "President Clinton and the Republican leadership in Congress are stalemated in federal budget deliberations, and all 'nonessential' government employees are on indefinite leave. This includes those people who process passports. I may not be going to Switzerland, after all."

On Tuesday, January 2, Susanna and I went to see Terry Gunderson, constituent aide to Congressman David Obey, in her office in Wausau. Ms. Gunderson's initial advice (she was swamped with people in passport trouble) was for Susanna to call the Swiss Embassy, to see if I, as the husband of a Swiss citizen, could be admitted to Switzerland, in an emergency situation, without a passport. Later that day, Susanna had a charming, polite, witty and utterly unproductive conversation, in Swiss German, with a ranking member of the Swiss Embassy in Washington, D.C. His answer, of course, was no, of course not.

And then Rhonda, on her own initiative, decided to work the phones. After several near dead ends, she reached a Mr. Keading, in Field Operations at the State Department, also in Washington, D.C. Putting Rhonda on hold, Mr. Keading called me and, with a fine voice of grumpy condescension, told me to do three things: authorize Rhonda, via notarized letter and overnight mail, to act as my agent at the passport office in Chicago; include with the authorizing letter a photocopy of our airline tickets; and get a physician in Switzerland to FAX Rhonda a letter spelling out Mama's actual physical condition.

By Friday, January 5, Rhonda had most of this paperwork in her possession. Terry Gunderson phoned me to say Congressman Obey had used my name and my predicament in a speech on the House floor, arguing for reopening the government. She asked if I wanted a copy of the *Congressional Record*. I laughed and said, "No, all I want is my passport."

Congress *did* vote to temporarily reopen some government offices, including those that process passports. These were scheduled to open on Monday. We immediately realized that this compounded our problem: it was one thing for Rhonda to walk into a virtually deserted office with all the necessary documents, and it was quite another to be part of a tourist mob, each person clamoring for attention, in a wild futures market for passports.

The phone rang shortly after two o'clock, Monday afternoon. Rhonda, calling collect from the Art Institute, said she had in hand my very own passport—and her story was rich with determination, perseverance, and last-minute good luck. The offices, the waiting rooms, the hallways, corridors and elevators, everything and everywhere was packed with people, a virtual zoo. Only Rhonda's stubbornness saved the day.

To say Susanna was relieved is to seriously understate the case. But fate wasn't done toying with us yet.

On Tuesday afternoon, I was called by Meg Dedolph, a news reporter for the *Wausau Daily Herald*. My story, such as it was, appeared in Wednesday's newspaper. In it I threatened to send

House Speaker Newt Gingrich my long-distance telephone bill.

On Thursday, January 11, our friend Charlie Green, his nose no longer crooked, drove Susanna and me to Central Wisconsin Airport. We were proud of being early, having left home in plenty of time to make the 12:59 p.m. flight to O'Hare. We sauntered up to the ticket counter and were immediately told our flight was cancelled and that the last flight to Chicago would leave in exactly ten minutes. Needless to say, we hustled. Charlie, in his red coat, stood waving outside the chain-link fence as our plane lifted off.

But our plane did not go directly to O'Hare. We flew east, and landed in Green Bay. It was cloudy and snowing and getting worse. We went into the terminal and sat. We reboarded the plane, rolled to the runway, and sat. Periodically, the pilot would inform us that weather conditions in Chicago continued to be rotten. Not all runways were open. Priority was being given to incoming international flights. Therefore we waited. And sat.

We returned to the terminal. The pilot told us that those who wanted could go inside, that our flight (also the last from Green Bay) wasn't cancelled, *yet*. Susanna went into the terminal and learned that the flight to Zürich from O'Hare had been postponed from 4:45 to 7:45. We hoped that Rhonda, still in possession of my passport, would not give up. I read the second chapter in E.F. Schumacher's book, *Good Work*, with its insightful criticism of technology, size, and speed. I squirmed in my seat.

And then we did take off and flew south at 10,000 feet, the sun an inch above the southwestern horizon. In the domain of angels, the stewardess with the red sweater served drinks.

We had another bout of panic at O'Hare. We couldn't find Rhonda and Imtiaz. We couldn't reach them by phone at work or at home. After a good half-hour of nervous sweating, we were beckoned to the Zürich check in counter (we'd already been there, and the phones were close by). We were told that Rhonda and Imtiaz were on their way from our *arrival* gate. Within fifteen minutes I had in hand my very own passport and Rhonda was gasping for breath under the smothering gush of our gratitude and relief.

We had a quick meal with Imtiaz and Rhonda—these wonderful

young people—and were on the 767 by 8:04 p.m. (The flight had been delayed again.) It was 9, or later, before the plane was deiced and we were headed to the runway.

At 4:27 a.m., U.S. Central Standard Time, I could see out the airplane window little villages, small towns, fields, roads, and a long shoreline with microscopic surf. When I asked the stewardess whether this was the south of England or the west of France, she said she didn't know. And, frankly, she didn't seem to care.

Saturday night
January 13, 1996

The land we saw Friday morning, far below, was France, not England. With the pampered arrogance of imitation gods, we ate a continental breakfast over the heart of Napoleon's empire. But the plastic dishes were cleared away before we circled repeatedly over the Zürich area.

I was enchanted. There were massive snowcapped mountains far to the south. Directly below were fields and hills and ravines, forest in larger chunks than I somehow anticipated, villages, a castle, a large river (the Limmat, Susanna said), everything so neat and nice. The colors that predominated were extraordinary shades of grey-green and brown, terribly inviting. I began to feel as if we were flying over the Hobbits' Shire, that literary creation of J.R.R. Tolkien, and I almost began to wonder whether Swiss people were extremely short, with hairy feet. (I asked Susanna to take off her shoes and socks, but she only looked at me with indignation.)

The most eerie things were two huge smokestacks emptying effluent into the sky *above* the fog: Susanna's father told us, later, that these were not smokestacks but nuclear power plant steam vents.

The plane, as it circled, had been steadily losing altitude. We dove into a bed of fog and rolled up to the Zürich terminal—which is actually not in Zürich but in Kloten, maybe ten kilometers northeast of Zürich. (And a kilometer, I might as well say now, is 0.62 miles, according to my *Webster's*.)

Dicker Nebel. Dick is pronounced "deek," meaning thick or fat. *Nebel* is "nay-bell" and means fog. Deek Naybell, that will be my Swiss pen name. Deep Fog.

Now lots of things that, in English, don't have gender, in Swiss German, do. *Nebel* is male. So Deek Naybell is not a total disguise: just your normal American fellow walking around in a typical deep fog. Tired but wonderfully alert, we did the necessary things at the *Flughafen*, literally the "flight port." Pass through customs—Susanna with her Swiss passport, bright red and well-used; I with my crisp new blue American. Wait for our luggage (two suitcases and my guitar, safely encased and not too badly scuffed). Exchange dollars for *Franken*. (The rate was 1:1.12, or $100 bought Fr.112. Susanna said that when she left Switzerland in 1969, Fr.480 bought $100. So here's a little mathematical quiz: Guess which country's currency has taken a beating in the last quarter century?) Pass through a second checkpoint which, momentarily, we thought would be a major luggage examination. (It wasn't.) Buy two train tickets to Sulgen.

By the time we stood on the train deck, deep below the *Flughafen* proper, we had walked a long way, taken three descents on escalators (holding firmly to the shopping cart sort of thing our luggage rode in), exchanged tapes with a panpipe player, Octavio Ramiro Rivera, from Bolivia, who was the only "street" musician we saw. But then there were two remarkably young policemen, each with a pistol and a club, one with a machine gun slung over his shoulder, both a symbol and a reminder of deadly violence in the world. And as we walked we simply watched people, the universal airport entertainment.

Susanna, who has been busily making our bed while I sprawl here writing, tosses me an old Swiss map. On it, in a corner, in Susanna's handwriting, are these facts: Wisconsin—56,154 square miles; Switzerland—15,941 square miles. So Switzerland is between a quarter and a third the size of Wisconsin.

After I helped a young woman zip her little blond dog in a glorified bowling ball bag, complete with plastic window and air vents, the electric train came whooshing/roaring in, and we struggled aboard a green second-class coach, not at all crowded, and sat down. Quickly the train (maybe eight coaches in all) whooshed/roared out, and in a very few minutes we were out in the sunshine, headed east and a little north, through the neat, neat, neat Swiss countryside.

There were long, skinny plots of community gardens in odd-shaped wedges of land adjoining the railroad tracks. Patches of woods, largely spruce, pine, and beech. Some newly planted trees. Tiny fields that came virtually to the rail bed. No snow but for clumps in deep shade. Tidy, practical houses and villages, some occasional old farm building. (But when I say old I don't at all mean dilapidated. The only ugly things I've so far seen were the mammoth vents belching whatever into the sky above the fog, and an obscenity in English chalked on a wall within sight of the train window—but also "FREE MUMIA ABU-JAMAL!")

We changed trains in Weinfelden ("wine fields")—never leaving the station platform because the next train came so soon—and when we got off the next train at Sulgen, there, across the intervening tracks, standing very still, in a long, green wool coat, beaver hat, and enormously bushy black eyebrows, stood Vater Andreas. We hurried down, under, and back up the far side. There we hugged and kissed cheeks, like good Russians.

Mama Irma, Vater Andreas, and Susanna in Mama's nursing home room.

Within five minutes—well, maybe ten—we were in Mama Irma's ground floor room at the nursing home, more or less across the street from the train station. Mama was curled asleep on her right side, facing a plain wooden wall. Vater gently woke her, and at first she was confused, thinking Susanna was Julia. But the confusion soon

The Buchenberg.

passed. They hugged and kissed and exclaimed their greetings over and over. When my turn came, I held Mama's left hand between both of mine, and I was instantly aware of fragile, brittle bones. I was actually afraid I'd pressed too hard and had hurt her; but she showed no sign of pain. (Today I was almost too timid to take her right hand, for fear of her bones.)

After a short visit in Mama's room, Vater and Susanna and I piled in Vater's car and drove here, to this odd, big house, with plenty of daylight left in the sky. *Götighofen* is the village. *Buchenberg*—"beech mountain"—is the hill, the street, this house. We had a tour of the house, some lunch, and we chose a third-floor bedroom to move into, partly for the roominess, partly because it's cooler, but largely to get as much distance as possible between our lungs and Vater's loooong cigars: five or more cigars each day multiplied by (let's say) seven inches per cigar multiplied by roughly sixty years adds up to a heap of smoke. We are not, so to speak, holding our breath that this is a habit to be given up any time soon.

We tried the bed for a nap and were happy to report that it worked fine.

Susanna did manage to eat as she not only conversed but

translated, the conduit of words between Vater Andreas and me, the weather prognosticator of windy speech between Vater with the scarred, bald pate, bushy eyebrows, and m i s c h i e v o u s eyes, and Deek Naybell, his

Vater Andreas and Susanna.

amerikanischer fogmeister son-in-law. *Gell?*

Sunday evening January 14

The phone rings—loud!—as I sit to write. But I won't go down to get it. *Gell?*

Gell is rather like the American OK, a versatile word which is the Swiss way of saying the High German *gelt*, meaning "Is it not so?" It can also mean "You understand, don't you"—either as question or statement. OK? *Gell?*

Five o'clock, dim light, foggy. Susanna and I were out for a pretty good walk; now she and Vater (V and F have an F sound in German; the very beginningist of students will stuff his shirt with hot *Nebel* and posture as a teacher) have gone again to see Mama in her small, comfortable, rather stuffy room in the nursing home. We were all there for the noon meal today—a good meal, served as if we were in a restaurant, of cauliflower with sauce, a Swiss dumpling called *Spätzli* ("little sparrow"), salad with two kinds of lettuce, tomato, shredded radish, and slices of cold, steamed carrot, a very tender beef in gravy, wine, water, coffee, and, for dessert, coffee ice cream with raspberries!

Talk! Talk! Talk! Always talk and more talk. Vater Andreas and I wear our poor Susanneli down with words needing rearticulation. This morning, at breakfast, the subject was largely Yugoslavia: the war, the U.S. and European powers as peacemakers, Russia as the perennial restless bear, the language of Albania...At one point Vater got up to mimic a conductor from Montenegro directing an orchestra—crouching, springing upright, wild gestures, theatrical facial expressions—a pantomime of Balkan temperament.

We laugh a lot, mostly at ourselves.

When I get my hands on the appropriate book, I will write a little about birds: the one we occasionally see with a long tail rather like the magpie of the American west; the crows that look very much like our crows but which have a somewhat different call. ("They roll their R's," I joked to Susanna on our walk this afternoon. "Ours say 'caw', these say 'carrrr.'") The chickadee-like bird we saw in the bushes outside the nursing home today.

Mama ate remarkably well. And she walks, or walks/shuffles, quickly from her room to the elevator, and from the elevator to the dining area. But she is uncertain, wobbly, and stiff getting up and down from her chair.

After the meal, back in Mama's room, we looked at our wedding pictures, the ones Bob Seitz took at the Methodist church in Merrill. And I paged through an art book of the late nineteenth-century painter Giovanni Segantini, whom I had never heard of before, and whose expositions of Swiss peasant life in the Engadine (that valley in southeastern Switzerland through which the Inn River runs) are simultaneously beautiful and realistic.

It is two kilometers to Sulgen from Götighofen. Vater drives his grey, four-door Nissan, and not slow, either. Yesterday Susanna and I walked here from the nursing home, a mostly curvy, uphill stroll with pastures, fields, patches of woods, vineyards, and orchards on both sides of the asphalt road. The tiny village of Gutberthausen is also on the way here, at the intersection of another narrow asphalt road that comes from the west, from Kradolf, a town along the Thur

Götighofen

River, south of Sulgen.

There is so much to see. My eyes feel bigger than my head.

Götighofen and Sulgen are in the canton of Thurgau, in the extreme northeast of Switzerland. (There are twenty-six cantons in all, some relatively big and some tiny indeed.) A canton is politically equivalent to a state in the U.S., even though the size of cantons more closely approximates a county. Thurgau, Susanna says, is probably the chief agricultural canton. And, indeed, the fields, orchards, and vineyards come right to the roads' edge: and the main roads are asphalt, narrow, with dotted white lines down the middle, each road edge paved with a single row of cut cobblestones of a uniform size (say six inches by four inches) which rise above the roadbed by maybe two inches. To walk along the road in traffic is to hug the fence line while the oncoming car whooshes past at a distance of maybe two feet.

Water, says Vater Andreas, is pressurized by gravity from a nearby reservoir, on a hilltop but underground, constantly replenished from wells. This house is hooked into a sewer system which goes, I believe, all the way to Sulgen. Likewise, there is a storm sewer system along the roads (the raised cobblestones are a kind of curbing) and even storm sewer grates in low spots on gravel lanes through vineyards!

The overall effect is of a lived-in park, with little gullies, streambeds, and steep hillsides of wild woods. Houses and barns are often long, continuous buildings: I've seen some that are probably two hundred feet in length. There are timber-frame houses, old, with white stucco; barns with huge overhanging eaves buttressed by beams; tiny gardens with no wasted space; old iron grillwork on windows and garden fences; incredibly wide house doors of ancient lineage, without windows, thick and weathered and ornamented; little poems on house walls telling how God not only made grapes for wine but human thirst, as well.

Even the manure piles are neat, each set in a concrete crib.

I've seen a few cows through barn windows. Sheep—a dozen here, a dozen there—graze in fields or pastures, some quite tiny, some with large, old fruit trees growing here and there. A few geese. A dog or two. A couple sleepy, watchful barn cats. Chickens pecking and scratching about the farm buildings.

No junk. No garbage or disorder. No shabby buildings, and no discard machinery rusting away behind a tumbledown shed. Although it's certainly premature to generalize about Switzerland as a whole, my hunch is that this sense of order pervades the entire country. Perhaps some day I'll know.

Monday afternoon
January 15

Swiss *Nebel*, as usual. Apparently God was gracious the day of our arrival, letting us actually *see* something.

Vater Andreas has gone to see Mama. Susanna is fixing the noon meal, which is the big meal in Switzerland. And I sit on the couch in the music room. This is the largest room in the house, say thirty feet by fifteen. Vater's shiny black grand piano (a C. Bechstein) is in here, and a two hundred year-old tiny pipe organ in a closed wooden cabinet. A walnut wardrobe, closed, filled with music books. A round wooden table with photographs and some music paraphernalia. A light brown marble fireplace with MCMXXXIII cut into its face, and a hammered brass shutter, closed. A bookcase with art, music, and photo books. At least seven paintings on the walls, all originals, mostly by Carlos Schneider. A parquet floor. One large and two small modestly worn rugs, all colorful, with red predominating. A dark blue wallcloth with a white flower design covering part of three walls. White plaster ceiling. Tall, rather massive windows in two walls with brass latches and black marble sills. This light brown couch, four chairs, a black wooden music stand, two tall plants in the window directly behind me, a couple sculptures, an inconspicuous record and CD player.

The house is heated by hot water radiators from an oil furnace in the basement. The radiator in this room is hidden behind a wooden grill. Everything is solid and modestly elegant. All rooms have doors—windowless doors—that close and latch and lock. In general, rooms are closed when not in use: this is typically Swiss, Susanna tells me. The woodwork is not painted. No radio. No television. Traffic is very light on the dead end road. A feeling of stillness pervades. For the restless soul this would be a prison to rage against. For the tranquil soul it

Vater Andreas at the old organ.

offers repose and peace.

There is talk here, laughter, even clowning. But there is also serious discussion (which can erupt in laughter at any moment) and music that stirs the heart like the slow undulation of angels' wings.

Last night Vater Andreas played Bach for us....

From every window of this house one can see field or vineyard or orchard. We drove to a farm for apple juice this morning and bought twenty-four one-liter green glass bottles (returnable) for Fr.32.00. We then drove to a farm right in Götighofen for eggs and apples. Two eggs cost Fr.1.00 and five kilograms (a kilogram is 2.2 pounds) of apples cost Fr.5.00. Vater said the apples were a real bargain but the egg price was standard.

We were in bed by 10:30 or 11 last night; pretty hard mattresses on the floor with flannel sheets, wool blankets, and two feather beds—really two giant cloth sacks stuffed with down and feathers. These latter make us too hot, but we'd be too cold without them. So we find, by trial and error, how much of a foot, leg, hand, or arm to let out in the cold air, in order to radiate excess body heat.

We both woke in the night to lie in our thoughts for quite a while before we talked. I thought of Mama, old and frail, on the final turns of her life's footpath. I thought of Susanna's youngest daughter, Gwendolyn, as the personification of youth: yesterday, looking at photographs, Vater Andreas called her "dangerously beautiful." And I considered how youth looks at old age as freakish and repulsive, as if old people constitute a remote species; and yet how soon, so very soon, we are all there.

later

Back on the couch after a big meal (Vater, back from the nursing home, sat with us, but he had already eaten with Mama) and lots of talk. We played round the edges of the significance of art in contemporary society—noticing, for instance, how much more difficult it is now to name a major living novelist, poet, painter, or composer than it was even twenty-five years ago. And we looked at books, one on *Volkskunst*, folk art, and another on the history of the Walser, a group or tribe, maybe, who entered Switzerland from the south many centuries ago, and from whom, maybe, the Juon family springs. There were lovely old photographs in this latter book of log buildings in villages high, high, high in the southern Alps.

Susanna comes in. She's walking into Sulgen to see Mama, and I'm going along. My dear Susanneli.

Tuesday morning
January 16

Ditto to *Herr Nebel*. He's a real hanger-on.

In our third-floor room—six-inch wide boards, plain and remarkably free of knots, on ceiling and walls—vertical on the walls. Four-inch boards on the floor. One large hinged window—actually two tall panes of glass, each in a wooden frame and hinged, looking (I think) north. I'm still a little fuzzy, or foggy, about cardinal points. *Nebelkopf.*

Susanna writes a card to Gwendolyn. Shortly I will write one to Woody—"da Voodee," as his name is spoken here.

Briefly I want to say that Frau Doktor Annemarie Frick, the Juons' old family friend, was visiting Mama yesterday afternoon when Susanna and I arrived, having driven up from St. Gallen. By the time Vater came, and Mama had her supper in her room, and there had been the usual avalanche of words (*Lawine*, pronounced "laveena"; in German avalanches are feminine), it was decided that Annemarie would join us for the evening meal.

Susanna made *Birchermüesli*, a kind of mush made with berries and uncooked oatmeal. Bircher was the name of a doctor concerned with healthy eating. So we might say that *Birchermüesli* is doctor's mush. Now *Bircher* is not "burr-chur," as we lipspeakers would say (Vater says you need to hold cold boiled potatoes in your mouth to speak English), but more like "boor-sure," and spoken in the throat. (In my opinion, if you want to learn to speak German, start a daily routine of gargling wet pebbles.) "Boor-sure-moos-li." Doctor mush. And good!

And then music and more verbal "laveena." Annemarie had to leave much too soon for my liking, for she is an engaging conversationalist who just happens to speak English very well. (She once worked at a hospital in Portland, Oregon.) But, unfortunately, Vater gets quickly restless and impatient when he can't understand what's being said (his most memorable experience in an intensive English-language school in London was setting off the smoke alarm with his cigar). So mostly *Schweizerdeutsch* it was.

But what I sat to write this morning—and we're both somewhat impatient to go for a walk—is something Vater said this morning at breakfast, under the usual barrage of my curiosity. I asked about the taxation system, how the federal state or cantons support certain established churches, how the garbage system works. It turns out that Vater buys a certain kind of plastic bag that costs Fr.3.40 *each*, and this is the only bag the garbage collectors will pick up. In other words, you pay your garbage tax, so to speak, when you buy from a regular grocery store these outrageously priced plastic bags with a volume of thirty-five liters.

Pretty clever. Very *geschickt*.

Wednesday noon
January 17

Last evening, coming out of the nursing home, I said spontaneously, "Hey! It'll be clear tomorrow." The air was colder and drier. "Oh, now you're a weather prophet," retorted Susanna, her voice drenched in grey dubiousness.

So let's just say God hit a compromise between the weather prophet and the oracle of fog. *Nebel* above but *klar*, so to speak, below.

So when we all went to Flawil this morning—dental appointment for Mama—we could *see*. We drove from Sulgen down through Kradolf and southeast along the Thur River (a wide but wadeable stream) to Bischofszell ("Bishop's cell"), and then more or less southwest to Flawil. This was slightly more rugged country, with a little more woods, but still quite thickly populated. Orchards, vineyards.

I am somewhat surprised, or puzzled, by the apparent small acreage given over to vegetable production, although I may be misunderstanding the situation because of winter cover crops that I am mistaking for pasture, winter wheat, or grass for hay.

There are lots of vineyards, row on row of grapevines hung on wire and supported by wooden posts. And it looks as if a lot of the newer orchards are dwarf trees, planted close together and in rather tight rows. But there are quite a few older fruit trees of the large variety; one often sees these in a field or pasture, one here, one there, as if they are the last survivors of an ancient orchard.

Susanna's come up to say lunch is ready.

later

Susanna made a delicious soup, with vegetables and rice. The bread we eat comes right from the grocery store but it is very good, not at all the spongy white stuff that we dare to call bread in the U.S. (Swiss people who've been to the United States snicker when they talk about American bread.) And *Wurst*! Hardly a meal goes by without sausage of some sort on the table; and cheese, good cheese, whose aromatic qualities one would consider *zweifelhaft*, doubtful or dubious, if sniffed unexpectedly on the street or on the soles of someone's shoes.

After lunch, I washed dishes and Susanna put things away. Now she's taken out the vest—her Swiss accent invariably makes it "west"—the "west" she's making for me, dark green, with bright red embroidery. And so we talk.

We talk about Mama's condition: her brittle bones, her occasional uncertain memory, her dim eyesight, her various medications, her occasional incontinence, her present feebleness. Will Mama improve or "recover"? Bluntly, how long will Mama live?

The apparent consensus of the Juon sisters is that Vater is too *ungeschickt*, unhandy, to nurse Mama at home, alone. Not that he's too unloving; that's not the question. And not that he's too rough.

He's just without experience in this kind, this degree, of nursing care. Plus he had a tumor removed from his brain (the scar makes an interesting pattern on his bald head) only two years ago, and he's on medication to prevent seizures. So he can't take care of Mama by himself.

And that leaves only two options: 1) Mama stays in the nursing home, at a reputed cost of Fr.6,000 per month, or 2) Mama comes home with someone besides Vater to care for her.

Who? For the first time, Susanna and I talk about our living here a year, with "da Voodee," taking care of Mama. This is a very big, and very difficult, idea to chew on. And I don't think we will come to a decision any time soon.

Thursday morning
January 18

The usual grey *Nebel*. The temperature is a little below 0° C. (The centigrade or Celsius thermometer was invented by a Swedish astronomer in the first half of the eighteenth century. His name was Anders Celsius. And that reminds me to say how often in the U.S. we ran across people who were wonderfully confused about Switzerland and Sweden: that they are the same country; that Swiss people speak Swedish, or vice versa. "My gramma came from Sweden and always spoke Swiss, but I never learned it.")

The temperature during the past week has varied remarkably little. And there's been no true lifting of the fog since the day we arrived. No wonder the pilot circled and circled, for he too must have been delighted to *see* Switzerland (or is this Sweden?) from the air.

The jay-like bird with the long greenish tail is an *Elster*. The crow that rolls its R's may be either a *Rabenkrähe*, that is, a raven crow, or a *Saatkrähe*, a seed or seedling crow. (This latter crow has a white bill, though; so I think the ones we're seeing are the raven crows, the black bills.) There is also—no joke!—a *Nebelkrähe*, a fog crow, which has a greyish back and breast. And the chickadee-like bird we spotted near the nursing home in Sulgen is a *Meise*, a titmouse, of which there are several types: *Sumpfmeise* or swamp titmouse; *Weidenmeise* or pasture titmouse; *Haubenmeise* or crested titmouse (this one, from the picture in Vater's birdbook, begins to look more like a nuthatch— nuthatches are *Kleiber*); then the *Tannenmeise* or firtree titmouse; the *Blau*-(blue)-*meise*; and, finally, the *Kohlmeise* or cabbage titmouse. Why this latter fellow with the black streak down his chest is a "cabbage" titmouse is a mystery to me; but I think this is the guy we saw, even though the drawing in the book made him a bit yellow on either side of his black necktie.

This *Vogel* (bird) book and another big, fat picture book of Switzerland (called *Naturparadies Schweiz*), which I've gone through rather methodically over the course of several evenings, are both products of the American *Reader's Digest*!

What this latter book has taught me is that, roughly, the northern half of Switzerland is the relative lowland: the northern half that runs from Geneva—bordering and, at that point, almost surrounded by France—on the extreme southwest, running to the extreme northeast which ends at the Bodensee, which is a large lake bordered by Switzerland, Germany, and Austria. (Austria has the smallest hunk of lakeshore, the southeast end only.)

Now here's another interesting thing: the Bodensee (also called Lake Constance) is fed primarily by the Rhine River, which originates in central Switzerland and which eventually forms the border with Austria and with that European superpower Liechtenstein. Now somewhere about eighty kilometers nearly due south of Zürich, as the fog crow flies, there is an east/west watershed, a very Alpish watershed. The river that goes west, or southwest, and then sharply northwest, is the Rhone. The Rhone feeds *Lac Leman*, Lake Geneva, is joined by the Arve River in Geneva, and then flows on into France, turning south toward (and eventually into) the Mediterranean. Its total length is slightly more than five hundred miles. The Rhine, meanwhile, flows east and then north toward the Bodensee.

North and south of these river valleys, where the rivers themselves are still relatively small streams, are the Alps—some of which we saw, snowcapped, as we circled over Zürich last Friday. (Zürich, by the way, is sort of northcentral—the way we'd talk, say, of

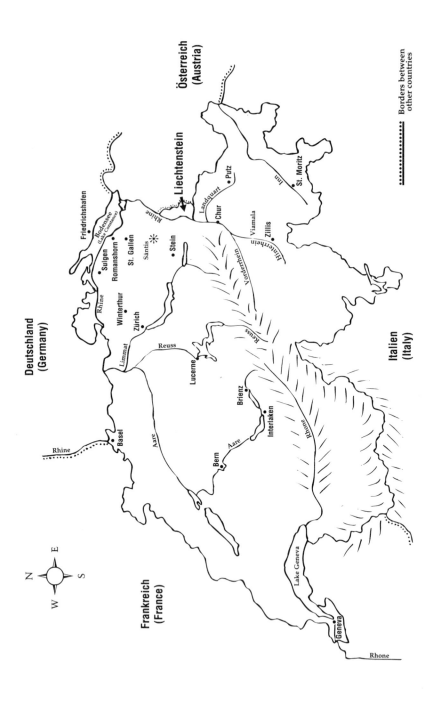

Switzerland

Deutschland
(Germany)

Österreich
(Austria)

Liechtenstein

Italien
(Italy)

Frankreich
(France)

N
E
S
W

Friedrichshafen

Bodensee
(Lake Constance)

Sulgen
Romanshorn
St. Gallen
Säntis
Stein

Rhine
Winterthur
Zürich

Limmat
Reuss
Lucerne

Aare
Brienz
Interlaken
Bern
Aare

Basel
Rhine

Rhine
Chur
Landquart
Putz

Vorderrhein
Viamala
Zillis
Hinterrhein

Inn
St. Moritz

Reuss

Rhone

Lake Geneva

Geneva

Rhone

Borders between
other countries

Wausau, in Wisconsin). And both north and south of the Rhone, high up, there are glaciers, real ones. I've seen 'em in the *Reader's Digest*.

So—hang in there for a little more fictitious political geography, these imaginary lines that divide *Mutter Erde* into chauvinistic little nation-states bristling with *Überlegenheit*, superiority.

We start with Basel, a large Swiss city in the northwest. The Rhine, flowing west out of the Bodensee, has been the border between Switzerland and Germany—*except* for the canton of Schaffhausen which crept north across the Rhine when Germany wasn't looking. (Schaffhausen *purchased* its freedom from the Habsburg family in 1418, and became a Swiss canton in 1501.) So, *except* for Schaffhausen ("work houses"?), the Rhine cuts a watery line, complete with waterfall, between Germany to the north and Switzerland to the south.

Now, at Basel, Switzerland, Germany, and France meet, so to speak, and we take leave of the Rhine, which flows north to divide these larger, ancient enemies, and which empties, full of gall in more than one sense, into the North Sea, after sprawling west through Holland.

So, *now* we can start with Basel and proceed southwest, in a crooked sort of way along this border with France, to and around Geneva. Here France does a little dance around Geneva, swings up from the south, and goes for a political swim in *Lac Leman*. But before the Rhone enters *Lac Leman* on the far southeast, France gets out of the water, shakes itself like a wet poodle, and heads south-southeast toward Italy.

And then about fifty kilometers south of the Rhone's watery mouth at *Lac Leman*, Italy asserts its imaginary line, and we begin to head east, in a jagged sort of way. This border is tumbled with Alps: Susanna says the highest peak in Switzerland is right on the Italian border, *die Dufourspitze*, 4,634 meters. Eventually we cross a long, big, skinny lake—Lago Maggiore—and head, jaggedly, to Switzerland's southernmost point, just a couple of kilometers from the Italian city of Como and thirty-five or forty kilometers from Milano.

We then go back north-northeast, near to a north-flowing tributary of the Rhine called Hinterrhine, then east maybe fifteen kilometers before the geopolitical roller coaster dives south-south-east again and all the previous lakes and mountains and rivers and glaciers begin to tumble ominously in our uneasy bellies. Hold on! Our border coasting is nearing its end.

A little east, back north (St. Moritz, where the late Shah of Iran liked to hang out, is less than twenty kilometers to the west), and just as we head east again we can catch a glimpse into the national park, swing north, bump into Austria and meet up with the Inn River, which is for a tiny while also our border with Austria. (The Inn flows northeast through the Engadine valley—Segantini country—before it enters Austria. It flows on through Innsbruck ("Inn's bridge"), and eventually joins the Danube, which empties in multiple channels into the Black Sea on the very eastern edge of Romania. Swiss water gets around.)

Vater Andreas and the author.

From the Inn, we head west in a crooked way—Switzerland on the south, Austria on the north—until we bump into Liechtenstein, all sixty-five square miles of it. Ten more kilometers west and we are back, truly bushed, to the Rhine. Here, if you're as worn out as I am from this border patrol, we can climb in old inner tubes and float north past Liechtenstein, then Austria again, until we get washed into the Bodensee. We'll hug the west shore, paddle in at Romanshorn, trudge the last ten or twelve kilometers to Götighofen, and collapse on Vater Andreas's doorstep.

"*Vater Andreas! Ein Becher, ein grosser Becher Slivowitz, bitte!*" (Father Andreas! A cup, a *big* cup, please, of plum brandy!)

Vater opens the door, the massive front door with no exterior latch, sees us sodden and gasping on the stoop, fetches his 840-pound Saint Bernard named Fritz von Bobo, and trots him out with a keg of beer strapped under his throat.

"*Danke schön*, Vater. *Wahnsinnig. Wunderbar.* Far out."

late
afternoon

The ceiling lamp (with three bulbs) is on in our bedroom. Susanna has gone with Vater to see Mama. I should go for a walk...

Truthfully, I miss the woodsy walks in northern Wisconsin. Partly it's the privacy, the sense of being alone. Partly it's being in undisturbed nature—the leaves, the birds, the gossiping brook. These are rather summery images, I know; but the price one pays for living in a glorified park is the lack of privacy outside the walls of your own house. Perhaps this explains the windowless doors on houses, and also the internal doors which are mostly kept closed: the greater lack of privacy outside results in a more formalized privacy within.

It's not that people here aren't polite. Quite the contrary. When Susanna and I walk, we are invariable spoken to by complete strangers, even people riding past on bicycles. Usually this is a formula greeting—"*Grüezi, mitenand.*" (Greetings to you together.) This is usually said to us with a face plump with curiosity.

The farmhouse where we bought eggs and apples the other day is right in Götighofen. Susanna and I had walked by there on previous occasions, and I had petted the dog, a big guy with a bum left leg, whose name (I eventually discovered) is Rico. Now when Vater was paying the *Frau*, she said she had seen Susanna and me walk past; and she told Vater she had been frightened by my appearance.

"Ooof," said Vater Andreas, *"Er ist nur der Kaiser Rotbart."* (He is only the Emperor Red Beard.)

Anyway, what I had in mind to write, before I got tangled up in gossipy beards, was something relevant to E.F. Schumacher's *Good Work*. I've just finished the essays—really the transcriptions of a number of talks given by Schumacher in the U.S., just before he died nearly twenty years ago. Now I'm nearly done with a long, final essay by Peter Gillingham, called "The Making of Good Work".

Schumacher, a British economist, was the reasonably famous author of *Small is Beautiful: Economics as if People Mattered*, one of the finest arguments I've ever read for smallness of scale and decentralization in economic affairs. But where Schumacher is chatty but substantial, in a *Brot und Wurst* sort of way, Gillingham is erudite with a cleaner style, more abstract, and *witzig* (witty). Both writers argue for people taking more responsibility in their own economic lives—self-reliance, disengaging from dependency on huge, power-driven systems, and to do this personally and collectively, in a small-scale sort of way.

But Schumacher's starting point satisfies me much more: our life-long task, he says, is to love God (and therefore also God's Creation), love our neighbor, love ourselves. Religious values and principles, in other words, must be at the core of our conduct. Without these values and principles, he says, boundaries are lost, everything is deemed possible, nothing is sacred, social, economic and political systems grow into immense forms simply because it is (temporarily) possible for them to do so. Undergirding this eruption of systems is the regimentation of human lives coupled with the plundering of natural resources, fossil fuels in particular, oil especially. When oil becomes too depleted, our standard-of-living mushroom will collapse.

Gillingham doesn't talk about God. His argument is that there are more smart, self-willed people now than previously, due in large part to better nutrition and the educational freeing up that's come with the Industrial Revolution, and smart people don't want to be limited by big, stupid systems that crunch self-expression and initiative. Yet at the end of his essay, Gillingham comes back to "the vertical dimension." Work then becomes "the place where our temporal and spiritual dimensions converge to create acts in the world." He concludes with a thought from Schumacher that he says haunts him: "If you know something, he said, really know it, and don't act on it, then it will go sour on you, it will fester inside you."

So in a very real and direct way, that's what all this ink is about. That's why I'm working hard, hard, hard to keep my eyes open in *der Schweiz*.

Verstanden? Der Kaiser Rotbart has a *metaphysisch Geschwür*, a metaphysical fester. He wants his work to be of service to God, and mostly he feels he's been a real *Nebelloch*, a foghole. Our task for and with each other is not to be befogging, but to be yeasty, helping each other bubble up to greater spiritual alertness and everyday cheerfulness.

If only *die Schweiz* could find a bubbly export market for *den Nebel!* Maybe that's my divine calling: God's fogpump in *der Schweiz!*

Friday morning
January 19

Add *Frost* to *dem Nebel* and you have a white Christmas, a little late, but complete *mit Engelhaar*. Frost is frost, except that Swiss *Frost* has a ripple in its R, with or without the angel hair.

My hair is less angelic simply because it's a lot shorter. I asked Susanna to cut it and last night, after supper, she did—*mit dem* lawn mower, pruning shears, and hedge clipper.

Die, das, der: she, it, him. So many things are gendered! Birds as a whole are male: *der Vogel*. But a particular species of bird—for instance, *die Amsel*—can be female. (The *Elster* is *die*; the *Rabenkrähe* is *die*; the *Kohlmeise* is *die*.) Owls are *die* as a whole; but a particular type, say the *Waldkauz*, is *der*. A lot of hawks, birds of prey, are *der*: *der Merlin*, really a small falcon. And then there's *das Haselhuhn*, the hazelhen, a type of grouse that because it's already a hen (*Huhn*), is therefore *das*. *Verstanden?*

There were three *Amseln* in the yard this morning—sort of the

Bischofzell

Swiss robin, says Susanna. Except for their size, though, they don't exactly look like robins. The shape is similar, but the male is black with a yellow-orange beak, while the female is more brownish, beak included.

So I'd like to introduce you to Mr. and Mrs. Swiss Family Robin, *die Amseln von den Vögel*. Compost thieves.

Mama has a 5 p.m. (really a 17:00) appointment *mit dem Zahnarzt*, the toothdoctor, in Flawil today. Susanna and I had planned to walk to Bischofzell this morning and explore the old, inner city—tall old houses, wall to wall, in a large irregular ring, with taller stone tower-gates here and there. We saw a little of this on our way back from Flawil on (when was it?) Wednesday—*Mittwoch*, midweek—but we couldn't linger long because Mama was tired and not feeling well.

But we are not feeling all that well, either. The crud we brought with us from America lingers on. At breakfast, I told Vater that *mit all dem Nebel* I have moss growing in my lungs.

Herr Nebel Moos Lunge at your (cough, cough) service....

Saturday morning
January 20

Two things about our drive to Flawil late yesterday afternoon. First, we actually drove *through* a patch of woods for a distance of maybe an eighth of a mile; even that little bit of *Wald* provided me with a peculiar relief from my forest withdrawal. Second, Susanna and I saw in a field (actually Susanna saw it first) a large wading bird. Because of our speed—nobody seems to drive slow in Switzerland— and the curvy road, we had one quick look, period.

This morning, after setting the table, I paged through the *Vogel Buch* and, later, with Susanna and Vater Andreas, narrowed it down to *der Graureiher*, the grey heron, *mit dem langen Schnabel*, with the big nose.

A word or two about Buchenberg. The main body of the village, Götighofen, lies in a hollow to the south, a stone's throw or two away. This house sits maybe halfway up the west face of the hill, with a semi-underground garage at street level and steep cement steps leading up to the massive front windowless door. (The flat cement roof of the garage is a patio on the west side of the house.)

In a horseshoe shape around the house is lawn and garden and grape arbor: the north side has the lawn; the east has the grapes, a semi-sunken greenhouse with concrete walls, and the compost bins; the south has several levels of terraced gardens, for flowers and vegetables. The entire lot is a quarter of an acre or less. A few trees.

There is only one house farther up the hill—immediately off the northeast corner of this lot, actually—and it belongs to Margrit Lässker, whom I've not yet met, who used to live here until her husband died: it was, in fact, her husband who designed this house and had it built. Beyond Margrit's house there is row on row of grapevines, carefully pruned and tended. This vineyard (we've walked around it) crowns the hill. Up there, too, is a small closed building alongside a heap of waste grape parts, skins and seeds, obviously the residue from squeezing *den Saft*, the juice, from *der Traube*, the grape.

Also: Vater Andreas bought me an American newspaper the other day (*U.S.A. TODAY*, for a mere Fr.3.20!) and I was touched by the death of Barbara Jordan, a former Congresswoman from Texas, who was on the House Judiciary Committee that voted to impeach President Nixon. She was ill a long time. Dead at 59!

Grey, grey, grey. Cough, cough, cough. Susanna's probably worse than I am today. What a way to vacation in *der Schweiz*.

That's the *Dummkopf Geschwätz*, the dullard gossip, for this morning. *Der Schwatzermund*, the blabbermouth, feels two sandwiches short of a picnic. My apologies to the hungry ants.

Sunday morning
January 21

It's not exactly foggy, but it is cloudy, as if *der Nebel* has merely climbed to a slightly higher elevation for a breath of fresh air.

Breakfast done; dishes washed; up to write.

Discussing lunch in the music room, Vater said there is an "antique" steak in the freezer. A fossil, perhaps? I asked. "Shot while saluting," was Vater's reply, using what's apparently an old Swiss expression for tough meat, all the while scrambling to his feet and saluting in a *Wahnsinnig* way—feet apart, toes pointed out, back straight but head thrust forward, left hand pressed to the side of his head, palm forward, a completely vacant look on his face. I was looking at Jaroslav Hasek's brave soldier Schwag, in person. The usual burst of laughter.

"Ah, she was probably a *Gletscher Kuh*," he said, a glacier cow.

"Oh, now I know where *Glacé* comes from," I replied—ice cream—trying not only for a play on words but also making an indirect comment on the "antique" ice cream Susanna had earlier dug out of Vater's freezer. They laughed.

Ah, well, the usual clowning.

Susanna's next older sister Irma, and Irma's youngest child Simon ("Sea-moan"), were here yesterday afternoon. They came to Sulgen from Lucerne by *Zug*, train, visited Mama in the nursing home, and then drove here with Vater. We talked, we ate, we looked at photographs from America. Simon, going on fourteen, is a husky boy with dark hair, a voice on the edge of changing, and a little earring in his left earlobe. He wore a dark blue sweatshirt that said, in red letters around a sunburst sort of emblem, "The nature can be saved by protection"—in English. Not "Nature can be saved" but "*The nature can be saved.*" This is Germanized English, for they would say something like "*Die Natur kann durch Schutz gerettet werden.*" But "the" nature is

Simon and Irma.

really *die* nature, which is one more way by which we know that the *Erde* is a *Mutter*—Mother Earth. *Verstanden?*

Irma ("Air-ma") speaks English rather well (she said her French is really much better...) but, as could be expected, most of the conversation goes in Swiss German.

I coaxed everyone into the music room after we'd eaten our *Suppe*, soup; and pretty soon we were all singing while Vater played the piano. This we did as long as possible, but not long enough, for it was soon time to pile in the car and go see Mama.

For Irma and Simon this second visit with Mama was brief, and they soon walked to the *Bahnhof*, the train station, and caught a westbound *Zug*. (Lucerne is southwest of Zürich by forty kilometers, more or less.)

Hey! Susanna's just come up with a fantastic announcement: they've closed *die Nebel Fabrik* for the day (*die* rather than *der* because "factory" is female, *gell?*), and some "luminous being" in the heavens is beginning to shine down on us! (Astronomy is a very primitive science here.) *Wahnsinning! Wunderbar!*

Die Sonne!

Yes, indeed! *In der Schweiz der Mond ist männlich.* In Switzerland the moon is male and the sun is female. The confusion has just begun.

Monday morning
January 22

One month from today we are to leave for America. With this weather pattern persisting, we will have exactly three more days of fuzzy sunshine. It is, in other words, once again *wolkig*, cloudy.

But it was *wunderbar* yesterday, with glorious *Sonnenschein* on our long walk (complete with *Blase*, blister, on the bottom of my right foot), all the way to an old castle, complete with moat, weathered drawbridge, and ducks paddling about in the dark *Wasser*.

We walked, briskly, probably eight kilometers in all: south through Götighofen to Heldswil, then east southeast to Zihlschlacht, which Susanna said probably means "destiny battle," and then east northeast through the woodsiest area I've been in yet, called Hudelmoos ("rag moss"), to the old *Schloss* which sits *at the bottom* of a hill on the western side of the village of Hagenwil.

That I emphasize its location—*at the bottom of a hill!*—readily suggests my surprise and puzzlement and amusement. Why? Because a castle is an armed house, a prehistoric tank, a submarine in a moat; and to put this pile of rocks with a wooden roof at the *bottom* of a hill is to invite your enemies to a hot dog roast, with the roof for kindling,

The castle in Hagenwil.

and your very own self as the weenie.

The *Schloss* itself reflects this haphazard, cheerful incompetence, for it is largely a heap of fieldstone, uncut, uneven, and neither plumb nor straight—the sort of place one could easily imagine Don Quixote and Sancho Panza retiring to, to plan their next military campaign against the woolly mammoths.

The upper level is of painted wood, red in color, and it extends out over the stonework by three or four feet, supported by wooden beams (also painted red) set at an angle in the stone wall. The overall effect is of bumbling charm.

My blister and the westering *Sonne* caused Susanna to exchange a Fr.10 bill for coins—in the restaurant up in the castle—and to call Vater Andreas from the castle pay phone. (Shades of the American cowboy movie "Blazing Saddles" where the wildly galloping band of desperados, led by Slim Pickins, suddenly confront an unattended tollgate in the middle of the sagebrush, and then mill around, sweating and thirsty and hot, while somebody rides back to get a bag of dimes...) We then sat in the restaurant—except for the huge tile stove at the back and the chatter in German, we might as well have been in Des Moines, Iowa—and had coffee, at exactly Fr.3.00 per cup! (We did not leave a tip.)

So Vater Andreas, *mit der Zigarre*, came boldly in his grey Japanese car to rescue his beautiful daughter Susanna and her lame husband *der Kaiser Rotbart* being held hostage in Don Quixote's greasy spoon castle, guarded by Sancho Panza asleep with the ducks in the moat.

We drove to Sulgen to see Mama, the Nissan bubbling with laughs.

Tuesday afternoon
January 23

The *Sonne* is almost shining. *Wunderbar!*
The good news is we brought Mama home, for the afternoon,

Mama and Susanna.

from the *Altersheim* —literally the "old-age asylum." Or, more discreetly, the nursing home. The first thing Mama wanted to see is how it looks, on the north side of the house, where a tree has been cut down and removed since she was last here, which is weeks ago, at least. Susanna walked Mama in, arm in arm.

Vater, Susanna, and I drove into Sulgen about 10:30 this morning, smoke still rising into the fog from a brush pile fire on a wooded ridge where some limited logging is going on. (I am repeatedly surprised by the high proportion of mature trees in the woods here. In the Hudelmoos, last Sunday, there were newly cut spruce logs lying right by the narrow asphalt road, some of which were thirty inches or more at the base. I know because I sat on one in a failed attempt to arrange my socks in such a way to give aid and comfort to my blister.)

Anyway, Susanna and I shopped in the Co-op grocery store this morning (in what way it's a co-op I don't frankly know), while Vater went to be with Mama. There were two interesting things about this store that could easily be duplicated in the United States. First, the paper shopping bags with handles (which you can buy there or bring with you) have childrens' art on both sides; on the side panels there are photographs of the children whose art it is, their ages, and from which canton they originate. That you reuse your bag is good conservation; that each bag has child art on it provides a certain esthetic attachment and maybe makes you want to use it again, rather than throw it away. Second, the young women at the checkout counters sit on high, obviously comfortable chairs that turn and roll. This seems to me a very humane improvement over the American system where women stand, hour after hour, until their shoulders grow right out of their hips.

So we carried to the nursing home two bags of groceries and a little potted *Primel*, primrose, a small plant with dark green leaves that look like a cross between butter crunch lettuce and kale, but not as rumpled as either. The flowers are a little larger than a quarter, with velvety red petals lobed rather like clover leaves, with a bright yellow star in the exact center. We entered the *Altersheim* on Floor 0 (Mama has a room on 1; the top floor is 4, with a back entrance through a long glass porch) and we quickly bumped into Yvette who, with her husband Robert, manages the place.

(Yesterday afternoon Susanna and I played for the residents, in the dining area. We were given a long and—even in the Swiss German I could tell—terribly flowery introduction by Robert. We played for most of an hour and, perhaps stimulated by Vater's bushy eyebrows, played very well, too.)

Anyway, last night before we went to sleep, Susanna and I talked at some length about our responsibility toward Mama and Vater. Can Vater take care of Mama at home? No. Could they find, would they even consider looking for, a reliable person to take care of Mama at home? Big sigh: not likely. So either we return (for a year?) or Mama stays in the *Altersheim*? Yep, one or the other; no other option seems likely. Is it realistic for us even to consider coming here to take care of Mama? Hummmm. We don't know.

So, this morning Susanna took the opportunity to sound out Yvette about a hired, reliable person to care for Mama at home. They carried on this conversation in Swiss German, but I didn't need a translation (which I got later, anyway) to tell me it wasn't a very hopeful talk. Their facial expressions, hand gestures, and general body language told me most of what I needed to know. Our quandary persists.

Because I'm so unimaginative today, I'll just talk about *Geld*, money. Susanna read to me some land prices out of a local newspaper—lots for sale for house building. The prices varied from Fr.250.00 to Fr.270.00 per *square meter*! And in the grocery store this morning, we saw a package of very thinly-sliced dried beef. Doing a quick, rough calculation, Susanna rounded it out to a mere $30.00 per pound....

As Marie Antoinette of the impoverished Habsburgs said of northern Wisconsin peasants, *"Let them eat Birchermüesli!"*

Wednesday morning
January 24

The usual cloudiness.

In the second floor bathroom, cigar smoke lingers like a bad dream, as if the very air has a hangover. I suck on cough drops called "Throat Scrubbers" and cough my dry little cough that accomplishes nothing, except futile exercise for my lungs.

Vater has gone to see Mama. Susanna and I have moved our musical instruments up to our bedroom, out of harm's way, from the music room. The cleaning woman comes today. Vater was gloomily cranky this morning, before breakfast. Susanna accused him of being under the cleaning woman's thumb, for he was fretting that things were too dirty and too disorderly....

This quandary of Mama in the nursing home (Susanna called Julia, in Germany, last evening; Julia says she and Irma have agreed, completely, that Mama in the nursing home is the best solution, and that Susanna will come round to that point of view, too) throws off all manner of tangential thoughts and conversations. For instance, Susanna asked this morning if I ever wanted to write "a book of how things could or should be"—an eutopian novel, in other words—and I told her about a story I used to toy with called "A Lesson in Arithmetic" that featured two kids whose adventures, in a *News from Nowhere* or *Ecotopia* sort of social environment, never could be defined in a straight line. But before long, Susanna was telling me her conviction that all children should learn in their childhood to a) grow flowers and vegetables in a garden, b) take care of and clean up after animals, and c) provide some degree of care and comfort to old, ill, or disabled people. Which was, of course, the normal run of affairs in the old rural culture of small farms.

No matter how we turn, or where, we are forever unreconciled to so much of the new, the fast, and the theoretically improved. Annemarie, looking at a photograph of our log house in Wisconsin, said, "You mean this is as a critique—ah, how you say it?—*criticism* of how things are, ya?"

Ya-ya, ist Wahr. But to what avail? Don Quixote doing battle against the computer chip?

Perhaps I am too much like Konstantin Paustovsky, whose partial autobiography, *The Story of a Life*, I am reading: "As a little boy I already loved parks and trees. I didn't break off branches and I didn't rob birds' nests. Perhaps this was because Grandmother Vikentiya Ivanovna had told me that 'the world is wonderful and good, and a man should live in it just as in a big garden.'"

Just as in a garden!

But we are such restless, unsatisfied beings. Unwilling to discipline ourselves in quietness, contemplation, and sufficiency, we tinker, tinker, tinker at making things "better," at producing "progress," at "rising above" nature, at making bio-engineering experiments on that other tree from Eden, the Tree of Life. And Christianity, having very largely accommodated itself to "progress," lounging in its recliner, fat and lazy, is ethically incapacitated. Youth rebels out of instinct but, lacking mature ethical support, falters and turns sullen.

This is at least part of the reason why we do not, in the United States, have a serious and prolonged public discussion on the condition of rural culture. We are so under the illusion that "progress" means good that we are in the process of allowing our society to fall apart even as new technological developments race to make each other obsolete. What does "cultural stability" mean in this context? Truthfully, we haven't a clue.

Thursday afternoon
January 25

The train to Lucerne (I will try not to talk about the weather unless I've something good, or new, to say) pulls into Winterthur. There are a few empty seats. Quite a few people get off, carrying packages and bags.

We are on our way to Irma's and Hanspeter's house. This trip has been planned for several days. Vater dropped us off at the *Bahnhof* late this morning. While he went to see Mama at the *Altersheim*, more or less across the street, Susanna not only bought us tickets but also, for us each, a month's half-price card for Fr.90.00 per person.

The discount card seemed iffy for a while, as the two men in the office argued about whether Susanna, as a Swiss citizen, (we had to show passports), qualified for the discount. So they each paged busily through fat books of regulations while we stood outside the thick glass window doing our best (it wasn't hard) to look bored, long-suffering, impatient, and superior.

Aha! At last the issue was decided in Susanna's favor, and we left Fr.269 in the little revolving door. They revolved back to us a discount card each (complete with photographs) and two round-trip tickets not just to Lucerne but to Brienz.

Interlaken ("between the lakes") is a well-known Swiss resort town, a place to part easily and quickly *mit dem Geld*, with your loot, in exchange for scenery, ski lifts, and ambiance. The lakes are Thunersee, to the west northwest of Interlaken, and Brienzersee, to the east northeast. Both lakes are fed by the Aare River, which originates in the same rumple of Alps that waters the Rhine and the Rhone. (The Aare eventually joins the Rhine, northwest of Zürich, at the watery border with Germany.)

We're pulling into the Zürich terminal. I'll gawk.

Saturday afternoon
January 27

Der Nebel is the usual consistency, but my crud has gotten thicker. I am on various homeopathic remedies, including chocolate, courtesy of Susanna's sister Irma. The biggest problem is the steady beating of the elephant heart inside my head. For this, I may soon resort to organic aspirin, courtesy of my suitcase and the U.S.A.

The problem with sight-seeing is how little time it leaves for writing; and the more the sight-seeing, the bigger the burden for the pen. Not only did Susanna and I wander around Lucerne (I should say a very small portion of Lucerne) on Thursday afternoon, before hopping a bus to Irma's house, we also made a round trip by *Zug*, yesterday, to Brienz. Stir all this liberally with chest crud, headache, and a revived blister on the bottom of my right foot, and you have all the necessary ingredients for a champion American whiner.

Brienz is probably less than forty kilometers from Lucerne—in a straight line, that is. The *Zug* route is remarkably straight, actually, until the Brünig Pass (from Giswil to Brünig the train climbed hard, twice, using a retractable gear device). Brienz is almost due west of Brünig; but because of the terrain, the train route drops southeast to Meiringen, upstream from Brienz and the Brienzersee, on the Aare River.

The Aare River valley is remarkably flat, a mile or two wide, and dotted with farms. (In Wyoming or Colorado, this entire valley might be one cattle ranch....) The river flows uniformly swift and rumpled, grey-green jade in color, making one somehow think of melting glaciers. The river from Meiringen to Brienzwiler (where we got off the train to walk to the Ballenberg) is of a surprisingly uniform width—say sixty feet—suggesting that it's been canalized.

An official at the *Bahnhof* in Brienzwiler pointed out the very narrow road that climbs a big, steep hill to the north. We walked up this narrow, steep road, slowly and puffing, until we entered the Ballenberg.

Was ist der Ballenberg? For those who know Old World Wisconsin, near Eagle, southwest of Milwaukee, with its historic collection of old buildings from different regions in the state, and from different ethnic groups, Ballenberg does or is a similar thing for Switzerland as a whole, but with a deeper and richer history.

We wandered through several of these deserted mini-villages, connected by narrow roads, through a large, heavily wooded, rugged and boulder-strewn natural park, with real Swiss ravens flapping overhead in *dem Nebel* and calling down good-natured, croaky

Ballenberg

insults.

"Bug off!" I shouted up to them. "Our ravens can at least speak English!" And I coughed, loudly, to show them how it's done.

There were houses and barns, two or three centuries old, a wooden granary, a sawmill set up to work off a real water wheel, sheds, a limestone burner. There were little pastures for sheep, cleverly fenced with poles and bent sticks, and very real Brown Swiss cows with grubby flanks standing in an old, grey barn.

later

Back down to our ground floor room (this is a three-story house with kitchen, living room and study on the second floor, bedrooms on the third) after a good lunch of boiled potatoes with cream sauce, cheese, olives, and salad. The flesh of the potatoes here is rather yellow. The flavor is strong and good.

And then I put bread dough into pans. This is the first bread I've made since leaving Wisconsin. I miss it.

Ah, yes. On Thursday I left the reader gawking in Zürich. Tough luck. The trains do not wait. They arrive and leave on the dot. The train stations in Zürich and Lucerne are big, grey, blue, efficient, clean in a dingy sort of way, with almost no place to sit. They are buildings for people in rapid transition, and they are designed to that end, to the max.

In Zürich, we left one train, walked quickly till we found the

Lucerne.

other for Lucerne, got on, left. No monkey business.

In Lucerne, we stashed our big luggage (at Fr.5.00 per article) in a special closed room in the basement. The old man who attended to us apparently took pity on us—looking exactly like what we are, down-at-the-heels Americans—for he let us deposit three pieces for the price of two. We thanked him profusely.

And then we walked.

Just as Zürich is located at the extreme northwestern end of a long, skinny, curving lake—the *Zürichsee*—that extends thirty-five kilometers or so to the southeast, so Lucerne is situated at the outflow of the Reuss River from another skinny, long, but more crooked lake called the *Vierwaldstättersee*. (For convenience, we will call these lakes by their English names, Lake Zürich and Lake Lucerne.) Now the *Bahnhof* in Lucerne is located right where the Reuss River flows out of the lake; and so for two hours, Susanna and I acted like tourists, crossing the river four times—twice on wonderful old footbridges, built with heavy timbers, roofed, with paintings every twelve feet or so fitted on beams and triangular in shape beneath the roof. Each painting came complete with verses, in German, detailing some important event in Swiss history or legend. We entered, briefly, a huge, magnificently ornate Jesuit church. And we strolled on rather crowded, narrow cobblestone streets, entirely free of motorized traffic, in stone canyons between wonderfully old buildings reeking of a modest antiquity. The buildings were, let's say, substantial. The shops were, let's definitely say, upscale and chic and—well, at one point we went past a restaurant that had the word "ambiance" included among the descriptive terms advertising its charm.

"*Ambiance,*" Susanna said, pondering, "I don't quite know how to translate it."

"You don't need to," I replied. "It means deep pockets with postured class."

By far our best contact came with two street musicians, accordion and guitar, who played long and well despite the cold. (The accordion player especially had such long, thin, *blue* fingers!) We dropped

Street musicians in Lucerne.

some money in the open guitar case and waited till they'd ended their tune. Susanna talked German to the guitar player, who was probably in his thirties, with a round face and high forehead. He was Polish, he said; the song was

French. When we left they broke out in a rather jazzy American tune—familiar, but I never pinned it down.

I was struck, too, by how few people dropped money into the guitar case. That, at least, is very like America....

It was growing dusk, and our bag of delicious *Maroni*, hot chestnuts, nearly depleted, when we got back to the train station. In the plaza in front of the *Bahnhof* busses arrive and leave. We found 73, bought two round-trip tickets from the driver, and lurched aboard, struggling with our reclaimed luggage.

Bus drivers act like bus drivers, I suspect, the world over: aggressive, rude, extremely competent. The bus was clean, the seats comfortable. But the bus was not warm: the engine does not run except for the actual travel. Roadside bicyclists were terribly crowded but never crushed.

It was easy for Susanna to find Irma's home, in this suburb of Lucerne. (But even here, as we climbed one long set of steep steps, coming up the hill, we passed an absolutely tiny fenced pasture for a single sheep, hardly bigger than a living room! When we went down those steps yesterday, on our way to bus and train, the sheep was in there, little bell tinkling away.)

(And in Sulgen, by the way, which is a town of at least a couple thousand people, there are barns with cows in them. One barn sits right next to a huge Protestant church: Protestant because it has a rooster on its steeple rather than a cross, as Catholic churches do. Does this mean that Protestants worship chickens in Switzerland? No. It's a reminder that Peter betrayed Jesus three times before the rooster crowed *kick-er-i-ki*.)

later yet

Already the fog seems more dim. Evening approaches. I will bring this to a close with a few random thoughts and observations.

On our way south to the Brünig Pass from Giswil yesterday morning, we noticed the frost getting thicker and thicker on trees, twigs, branches, and wires. I have never seen such thick frost. The branches of big spruce were bowed down by it. Fence wires were coated with it to the thickness of a farmer's finger. And it wasn't snow. It was frost—layer upon layer, probably—but frost nonetheless.

Had the sun been shining at Brünig, we would've hopped off the train. It wasn't so we didn't.

In the Ballenberg, before we took the crooked *Wanderweg* (official footpath) and walked to Brienz, we ooohed and aaahed over the beauty, the solidity, the integrity of the old buildings and the more-connected-with-nature life they represent. (Which is essentially why we live the way we do in our non-electrified log house in Wisconsin.)

And then we walked and walked, eventually visiting with Johannes Finkel, the fellow who made Susanna's violin bow, in Brienz, nearly thirty years ago. He took us on a tour of his shop, which has been in the family for three generations, showing us a Fr.250,000.00 computerized machine that roughs out the bows, and which can also rough out a violin. Finkel bows are world famous, but Johannes said he has to compete with cheap Chinese bows, and he's hiring a German violin maker to finish out the machine violins because the machine "needs to pay for itself."

We walked farther into the village and had coffee and a (shared) piece of pie (Fr.10.50) in a little restaurant

Susanna with Johannes Finkel.

overlooking the Brienzersee. Through the windows we watched gulls ganging up on the one which had found a hunk of food: given the prices, this was completely rational behavior.

Then we walked to the violin makers' school. The narrow

Buildings, old and new, in Brienz.

streets turned and twisted on a very steep hillside, house after house of dark brown weathered timbers, carved and ornate. There were stone walls and terraced gardens, here and there a tiny barn. I wasn't feeling at all well; but I was well enough to be overwhelmed with the craftsmanship and beauty. An entire village of woodworkers and woodcarvers!

Simon Glaus, the assistant director at the violin makers' school, took us on a tour. It is the only such school in Switzerland, has a dozen students, and the canton (Canton Bern) is thinking of shutting

it down because of "financial difficulties." The students were young, of both sexes, and intense. Simon Glaus was extremely cordial and sweet-tempered.

To think that Switzerland, repository for the world's loot, licit and illicit, cannot

Susanna with Simon Glaus.

Stone church in Brienz.

afford to keep a dozen kids making violins is, well, an obscenity. (Wasn't "progress" supposed to liberate us from drudgery so we could devote ourselves to quality craftsmanship and the fine arts?)

On our way back to the *Bahnhof*, we wandered by the house where Susanna used to live, when she was a student learning to make violins; past the big stone Protestant church and the massive parish house where Susanna would occasionally have a meal with the minister and his wife; past four boys sneaking a shared cigarette in an alley. We bought fruit, bread, and cheese in a grocery store, and as we sat on the bench by the *Bahnhof*, waiting for the train to come from Interlaken, the fog began to lift.

By the Great God Almighty! There *are* mountains in *der Schweiz*! There was a huge, massive beast of a mountain rising immediately behind Brienz, to the north; and across the lake, to the south, there was a whole bloody wall of them, rising, rising, rising into the grey sky! Trees on snowy crests stood out like exquisite *Scherenschnitte*, the scissor cuts for which Switzerland is famous.

When the train pulled out of the *Bahnhof*, my face was as round and flat as a pie plate, pressed tight against the window.

Mountains! American pieface in *der Schweiz*!

Monday afternoon
January 29

The usual recipe of suspended water particles. And, like *der Nebel*, the moss in my lungs clings like lichen on a soggy rock—if that's not too heavily an oxymoron. But nothing can be too outlandish, or even too contradictory, to describe the sheer obnoxious persistence of fog and gunk.

Of Hanspeter's and Irma's four children, Barbara and Simon, the two youngest, are still in school, and they come home daily for lunch. Barbara (not "Barb-ra" but "Bar-ba-ra") said eight out of twenty in her class were home sick; only five out of twenty for Simon.

At Irma's gentle prodding, Susanna and I have decided to stay here till Thursday, rather than return to Götighofen today. Neither of us is exactly well.

Susanna went to church with Irma yesterday morning. When she came back, Susanna said there were exactly eight people in the pews to hear the sermon. She also said the sermon, given in *Hochdeutsch*, High German, was formal, stiff, and boring.

Later, for lunch, the invited musical guests arrived: Phillip ("Feel-ip") and Martha ("Mar-ta") and their two young daughters. During the meal there was talk of how voters in Canton Zürich narrowly defeated a proposal, in a referendum, which would have put an end to tax support for certain churches. This subject soon became terribly bewildering. It seems that cantons may "establish" one or more churches that then become tax-supported. The two main churches which seem to enjoy this support are the Roman Catholic and the Protestant. But "Protestant" doesn't seem to mean any or all Protestant churches; only the Swiss Protestant seems to qualify. This latter church apparently is a blend of the theology of Zwingli and Calvin. (Huldreich Zwingli was born in 1484, at Wildhaus in the Toggenburg valley, became first a priest and then a reformer, and was killed in a Protestant battle with Catholics, near Zürich, in 1531. John Calvin was actually French. Born in 1509, he eventually settled in Geneva and, as a reformer, became something of a religious dictator before his death in 1564. But it's also interesting to note that in

Switzerland, as in Europe generally, the Protestant Reformation tended to succeed in the more urban areas, while Catholicism tended to prevail in the countryside. The major exception to this pattern of urban Protestantism and rural Catholicism was the more radical "Anabaptist" movement. The word "Anabaptist"—the re-baptized—was originally used by both Catholics and Protestants as a derogatory term, for the "Anabaptists" broke with the practice of infant baptism because they found no biblical basis for it. For this and for their other beliefs and practices—"symbolic" communion rather than "real presence" eucharist, pacifism, refusal to take oaths, voluntary simplicity, and cooperative living—they were persecuted by both Catholics and "mainstream" Protestants. So in a very real sense, there were two Protestant Reformations, not one; but the "Anabaptist" reformation has in general received less acknowledgment because a) it was largely a peasant and working class phenomenon and b) it demanded radical changes in everyday life and economic structure, not merely in surface behavior or "belief.")

Somehow the conversation shifted into a discussion of Big versus Little. The Swiss people are arguing about the European Union (which Switzerland is not a formal member of) with its push to create a single European currency (the "Euro"), which is to replace the present national currencies, beginning in 1999. Many people (Susanna's father among them) see this largely as an attempt by the big European powers—Germany and France, in particular—to pry open the consumer markets of the smaller nations and also to muddy the waters of Swiss neutrality.

Phillip was an exchange student in Riverside, California, in the early 1970s, when many of his classmates were destined to be drafted into the army and sent to Viet Nam. He returned to Switzerland, he said, *very* happy to belong to a tiny nation that could not play power politics on a global scale and that had not been at war since the time of Napoleon.

Then I was asked whether I thought Wisconsin would be better off as a sovereign nation. The question threw me. I found myself saying that the issue of "states rights" in the U.S. had its chief thrashing out over the issue of *slavery*, and that all arguments for localized sovereignty have carried this taint of reactionary race hatred ever since. I spoke of the federal principles of Jefferson and Madison; how the old northeast (Massachusetts, Connecticut, Rhode Island) dragged its feet heavily on the issue of westward expansion, after our Revolutionary War; but how, also, by the time of Monroe, the United States was already convinced of its "manifest destiny" to expand to the Pacific.

While I was blubbering out this not-quite-to-the-point response, I was dimly realizing how so many people, myself included, believe or tend to believe that localized and small-scale government will be illiberal, stupid, insensitive, and brutal, but that big government makes for great statesmen, noble principles, and visionary ideas that turn out to be imminently practical. So I was just about ready to take another bite out of that question, this time with less hesitation, when somebody shouted "Music!"

As the outlanders, Susanna and I were asked to lead off. And so we played "Ashoken Farewell", that old sounding but actually rather new folk melody composed by Jay Unger and used as the theme music for a public television series on the American Civil War.

Phillip played both violin and guitar. Martha played a small accordion and the *Blockflöte* or recorder. Perhaps the most whimsical moment was Phillip's playing—and singing, in his deeply accented English—Bob Dylan's 1960s protest song "The Times They Are A Changing".

Irma and Martha played some lovely classical duets on their recorders, and Simon hauled from his bedroom his bass fiddle and plucked out bass rhythms on folk tunes, Swiss and American.

Like all good times, this one too came to an end. But it was a delightful afternoon—harmless, entertaining, warm, thoughtful, and fun.

After Phillip, Martha, and their daughters left, Irma and Hanspeter (Peter is "Pay-tur") got a call from their second oldest daughter, Susanna. (The oldest is Rosemarie, a ski instructor and an apprentice in a drug store. She lives at home, but we don't see much of her.) Susanna is their only married child. Her husband's name is Haqi, and he is a Yugoslav of Albanian extraction. Susanna and Haqi wanted us all to come to their apartment in a suburb on the other side of Lucerne.

Immediately after supper Hanspeter drove us and we arrived, in the dark, at a big, square apartment building. Barbara stuck two fingers in her mouth and whistled loud enough to wake up the entire neighborhood. Susanna came running down to escort us up to the tiny apartment where she and Haqi live.

Haqi and two of his expatriate Yugoslav / Albanian friends were waiting for us—intense young men of medium stature, but wiry and strong, with very distinctive, chiseled features. All of them (Haqi the least) knew a little English. They shook hands with us and resumed sitting cross-legged on the floor.

First a fat book of wedding pictures had to be paged through. Then, with the three young men puffing away on American cigarettes, the talk turned to the plight of ethnic Albanians in Yugoslavia. None of these young men can go back—Haqi is in fact a deserter from the Serbian army—and Albania doesn't want them. So they are proud, humiliated, frustrated refugees living in a country increasingly tense about all the foreigners living within its borders.

They carried themselves like modestly tough, proud young men of the working class I knew in my Wisconsin youth, and I felt for them an immediate affectionate affinity. Their hopes for peace were not exactly strong. I wanted to ask one more question, just as that stir begins as guests reach for their coats.

"What will happen in Yugoslavia in a year or two?" The coats hushed. "War and more war," was the answer. "Between whom?" I asked. "Between the Serbs and Albanians in Kosovo," came the reply.

On that sober thought we departed.

Tuesday morning
January 30

Susanna and I have separate beds; but the bed I sleep in is bigger (it's Hanspeter's) and so Susanna often crawls in with me. During the night I woke to find her gone. This morning she explained: my fever was so intense, the heat was raising blisters on her skin. "You were like a furnace," she said.

But this morning I feel—I say this tentatively—somewhat better.

Everyone but Irma was gone by the time we got up. Freshly made juice, good coffee, bread and cheese waited for us on the table. I gently tossed questions Irma's way about the different places she's lived and where she liked it best.

"All of zem," she replied, smiling. And she proceeded to regale us with stories of the two French families for whom she was nanny, in the 1960s. The first of these were blue-blooded aristocrats who were slowly but steadily going broke trying to maintain, not only their house in Paris, but their *two* castles (Irma had pictures: the second castle was "only" a "hunting castle" in a vast forest. "Oh!" said Susanna, scrutinizing the photograph of this massive heap of stones, "just another hunting shack!") *and* a summer house on the Atlantic coast.

The second family was just filthy rich, owners of a factory that made light bulbs for Citroen and Renault. Their villa was in the south of France, on the Mediterranean, and the man liked to invite his pals, race car drivers. One driver, from Monte Carlo, had scars all over his body, Irma said. "Vell, I nezer zaw heem veisout hees sweeming zoot, so I deedn't know for sure about alls. All scars und no brains," she said, tapping her head.

Next door to this family was the villa of Jean-Pierre Rampal, the famous French flutist. Irma said she would much rather have been there....

There is a small, roofed patio next to the dining room. As I got up from the table I saw out there a small bird, about the size of a *Kohlmeise*, but delicate like a wren, with a pale red bib. I motioned to Susanna. She turned and exclaimed, "A *Rotkehlchen*!"

Her German took me completely by surprise. I thought she said, "A *roadkill*!" As if, instead of the little bird with the pale red bib that I was seeing, *she* was seeing a crunched race car driver from Monte Carlo with scars everywhere but under his swimming suit. I looked at her in pure astonishment, wondering which of us had the blister-raising fever.

later

I never did mention that, on our return from Brienz last Friday, we rode with, and talked the entire time to, two students from the violin makers' school, Philipp and Andi, who were going home for the weekend. Philipp spoke relatively fluent English, so mostly I spoke with him.

Both were rather small men, with small, strong hands. Neither was certain that making or repairing violins would be his lifelong career. This surprised Susanna, for she continues under the impression, utterly normal in her childhood, that when a man chooses a profession, that's that. Perhaps that tendency has changed—?

Somehow we got to talking about farming, about what a "small" farm is. When they found out I had grown up on a small dairy farm in northern Wisconsin, I had to explain that fifteen or sixteen cows was fairly normal, fairly average, then; but now anything under sixty, seventy, or even eighty cows is "small."

One thing led to another, and I ended up telling them, trying to explain to them, my anxiety over the radical modern tendency to chop off our basic cultural heritage at its roots (I meant rural culture but not only rural culture), apparently on the presumption that the old ways are utterly *kaputt*, not needed, unnecessary, a hindrance, and dead.

They listened attentively and I think with some sympathy to this point of view (for they too are in this dilemma: learning to hand-craft violins while, up the road, a man with a computerized machine can chip out fiddles by the dozen), but in the end they shrugged. And maybe this shrugging conveys their uncertainty, and even their resignation, regarding the viability of their craft and career.

In the train, at Lucerne, we parted with shared addresses and warm handshakes. As Susanna and I walked to catch the bus, in front of the *Bahnhof*, I felt a warm and pleasant buoyancy—glad for this unexpected contact, this little spark of timeless relating in the larger world which, for the most part, could care utterly less.

Tuesday evening

Nearly 6 (or, as I should say here, 18:00) and nearly dark.

Simon practices his bass upstairs. Irma and Barbara are gone for cello lessons. Rosemarie and Hanspeter are not yet home from their respective work.

This is a busy household.

This afternoon, Irma took us along grocery shopping to Migros. *Was ist Migros?* It's a not-for-profit chain store that sells food and clothing. The store we went to also had a restaurant; but whether that's typical I can't say. Migros also has mini-markets on wheels, such as come from St. Gallen to Götighofen and other villages at very specific times and places. The peculiarity of Migros is that it donates one percent of gross sales to "culture."

After the trip to the Migros store, we went to see Beat ("Bay-ott") Gabriel, a violin maker. Susanna had a minor problem with her bow. Beat fixed it (for free) while they talked of Brienz and the violin makers' school. It turns out that Beat and violin makers from all over Switzerland converged in Brienz, a week or so ago, to discuss and vote on whether the school should remain open. Of course they voted *yes.*

Beat spoke no English; so Susanna translated my remark that the U.S. should forego one aircraft carrier and use the money to teach violin to lots of young people, thereby creating a greater demand for violins. Following the translation of my (not exactly) sarcastic remark, there came a sheer torrent of Swiss German.

Later, Susanna told me I'd hit a raw nerve, for Beat went on and on about a relative of his who makes airplanes "on the other side of the mountain," military airplanes, but he (Beat) can't even discuss such things with him anymore. Beat himself has served in the military—obligatory for all young men—but if his son chooses not to go, he'll stand by him all the way.

It was a very simple, straightforward, tiny store: guitars and a variety of stringed instruments of the violin family in the first room, nothing displayed with any attempt at "artistic" advertising. And, in the back room, a very tidy shop with workbench, tools, bows, violin parts. Beat stood easily over six feet, a little lean, dark-haired, unaffected, and earnest. It was almost disconcerting how he looked like and how temperamentally similar he appeared to be like our violin maker friend in Iron River, Michigan, Keith Davis.

As Irma, Susanna, and I left the shop, I remarked on the kindred intensity of Beat and Keith, as violin makers, as personalities.

"Yes," said Susanna, "and maybe that's why I'm not one anymore."

Wednesday afternoon
January 31

Irma knits; and, therefore, being Irma, she also spins her own yarn.

Irma spinning.

Barbara, Irma, Susanna, and I ate the noon meal (Simon was in bed, sick) and then moved into the living room for coffee. Irma, with her ageless female restless hands, pulled out her spinning wheel. The soft, grey yarn came so smoothly and fine from the raw wool, held in her left hand. The treadle rocked up and down, the wheel spun, the bobbin grew plump with yarn.

It took a remarkably short time to fall under the spell, under the enchantment, of the spinning wheel—a work so like the kneading of bread, repetitive and somehow given to meditative wandering, so elementally creative. Naturally both Susanna and I had to try to spin. And we quickly discovered, to our dismay, that Irma's perfect treadle rhythm and gentle hand motion are slowly learned skills. *Her* yarn came evenly and without a break. *Our* yarn broke, got clotted, wadded, and gobbed; the treadle began to spin the wheel in reverse. *Our* yarn looked as if it had been spun off the rear wheel of a moped in rush hour traffic.

The author "spinning".

But that spinning is an art of tranquility was as obvious as my incompetence. Even this short lesson—watching Irma, trying it ourselves—I am given a deeper insight into Gandhi: how spinning became for him not merely a token of village life and economic self-sufficiency, but also his meditation, all those years in British jails in India. (There is a story about Gandhi that, whether it's factually true or not, still illuminates the man's character. On being put into prison, he took up a book and began to read. A guard came into his cell, took the book away, and said reading was forbidden. Gandhi thanked him, took up pen and paper, and said, "Really reading is not what I need to do, writing to my friends has deeper value." In a little while, the guard was sent in again to take Gandhi's writing materials. Gandhi thanked him, assumed the lotus position, and said, "Writing isn't exactly what I should be doing, either. What I truly need to do is meditate for peace and spiritual clarity for India's sake, and for my own.") Spinning teaches self-control and calmness and patience. It is the critical cultural link between the sheep and the sweater, that exact moment when tangled nature is made humanly useable in an important domestic way. The thread of your life will spin smoothly out if you master the tangled impulses of your unruly instincts.

Susanna comes down, coughing, to say: Irma says if we want to go to the glassblowing factory (she wants to take us), it's now or never.

Off we go.

Thursday morning
February 1

It's 8:30. At 9, we'll walk down the hill with our musical instruments and suitcase, catch a bus to Lucerne, and get on a train to Sulgen. I'm better—truly!—but Susanna, I'm afraid, is worse.

So I have a half hour to write.

Irma took us south, through Lucerne and past the *Bahnhof*, to the glassworks, at the foot of Lake Lucerne, where both the lake and the town of Hergiswil terminate abruptly at a massive wall of trees, frost, and stone, through which tunnels are cut for automobiles and trains.

Here there is a new factory for high-quality hand-blown glass. First we went through a free museum (very clever with shifting lights, opening and closing doors, displays that lit up and then went dark, all in the language of your choice) which gave the history of glassmaking (Egypt, Rome, Venice) in olden times and then the history of glassmaking in Switzerland.

The fuel for the furnaces was wood. So glass was not a tree-friendly industry. In fact, the glassmakers would have to pack up and go to a new valley after a few years, having consumed all the local forest of beech and oak!

Thursday evening

At Sulgen, in the *Altersheim*, we had time to drink coffee with Mama and Vater (Irma's and Hanspeter's children say "Mumee" and

"Papee"); to greet once again little, grey Tante Emma Hut, who gave us each a box of chocolates, and who is related to the Juons through the marriage of Vater's sister Elsbeth; and then we drove, Vater and Susanna and I, back to Götighofen, Vater holding in his mouth the entire time an unlit but half-smoked cigar, his perpetual stinkfuse.

"*Willkommen auf Götighofen,*" said Vater as we drove past the upright railroad-crossing arms, on the road to the village. Then, over his shoulder to Susanna (who was sitting in the back), he asked how he would say that in *Amerikanisch*. But I caught his meaning and, without waiting for Susanna's translation, replied, "Welcome to Götighofen."

"Velcomb tooo Götighofen," said Vater Andreas with a goofy face and the cigar poked up at an improbable angle. We all laughed, the slight formality of our return dissolved, and everything became familiar and normal.

Back in the big house, we put our luggage away; I chopped sausage and vegetables; Susanna made a soup. We ate the whole thing (only bread and coffee for breakfast), read three fine letters from Wisconsin (not only did the temperature drop to *minus* fifty Fahrenheit—named after the German physicist Gabriel Fahrenheit, who lived from 1686 to 1736—it also plunged sixty-five degrees in four hours, starting from forty-four degrees and heavy rain! Will I ever again complain about fog?), and took a nap. I woke from a dream—Konstantin Paustovsky's magnificent autobiography is subverting my *amerikanisch* soul—in which my daughter Hannah came home with a wildly extroverted, cheek-kissing Russian husband, home to the log house, and we had a lovely, big blue rug on the floor, with purple and green in it. Everything felt good and happy and alive.

Also! Aha! This is another good Swiss German word, indispensable, pronounced "allzo" and meaning "Well, then!" but also "thus," "so," or "therefore." *Also* we got up. Susanna went down first and called to me, "Come look!"

Out the west window of the second floor, we could see the orange sun, as wet and sticky as a cough drop, hovering in haze over the hill on which great clouds of grey-white smoke were rising from brush-pile fires. The tiny fires at the base of these shifting pyramids of smoke were as orange as the sun, flicking their little sticky tongues.

As if that wasn't enough, Susanna then called from the bathroom, "Come and see this!" And there, out the east window (Susanna had both inner and outer panes flung open), was a milky moon, gauzy and misshapen as a young cheese, on his way to his first dance.

I couldn't believe it! How does Vater Andreas, even with his wickedly shaggy eyebrows, conjure up *both* sun and moon in one afternoon as a little welcoming gesture? *Wunderbar! Also!*

later

Also, we left the poor glassmakers this morning without a new forest to burn down. Well, clever fellows, they put their new glass factory—early nineteenth century, if I remember the too-rapid museum narration correctly—at Hergiswil, seven or eight kilometers south of Lucerne, and right on the lakeshore. Now the furnace fuel, the firewood, could come to them by water, and from a very large area of woods all along the lake.

And so the glassworks lasted till after World War II, was not able to compete with automated glass factories, was closed and eventually demolished in 1975. Shortly thereafter, a master glassmaker by the name of Roberto Niederer was persuaded to start a new factory of hand-blown glass; then he died, and his ashes were strewn over the Ionian sea; then his son Robert took over and continued the business.

With that, and a little more razzle-dazzle light effects, a last door opened and out we stepped onto a huge balcony above the glass furnace itself, a massive self-contained thing with small doors that opened to a soft, liquidy, intense glare of pinkish-orange light: molten glass. Men with hollow rods that were maybe six feet long stood on a plank platform by the furnace. They thrust their tubes into the pinkish light, rolled them gently, and pulled them out, with a small pinkish-orange glob on the end, glowing.

They then blew into the tubes, and the molten glass puffed and swayed. They rolled the tubes, shaped the molten glass in water and in forms (which closed and opened pneumatically), blew again, rolled again, blew air onto the glass from nozzles; and when the piece was as it should be, always a little less orangish-pink, it was laid ever so gently on a pad, the tube tapped just so, and the glass piece came free. The pieces (there were five teams of workers, sixteen men in all) were handled and finished in various ways by men at a lower level, maybe three feet below the plank deck, and then placed in a slow-cooling oven beneath the balcony on which we stood. The men worked without haste but also without wasted motion. That everybody knew his job and knew his neighbor knew his job was attested

to by the complete absence of protective clothing. They wore casual street clothes. Several men wore sandals. One wore shorts. Not a burn or scar could I see. Nothing could speak more eloquently to their skill, confidence, and trust.

Suddenly, they all took a break. So we, too, wandered through another museum of glass, some of it wonderfully playful, literally so, for there were percussion instruments of glass

Susanna at the glass factory in Hergiswil.

(and little padded hammers to play them with), glasses whose rims could be rubbed with wet hands and thereby played, and—our biggest laugh—a round pane of extremely thick glass behind which we each went, in turn, making faces of extraordinary distortion to the remaining two, all the while laughing uproariously.

We went back to watch the glassblowers, really a delight and wonder to see. Once in a while, one or another of them would casually glance up to see what gang of monkeys was now hanging over the rail, gawking down; but their attention was on their work, on the glass, on the molten light.

Irma said, "Let's go." So we crossed the street and went to the glass store. Here she bought nine big glass marbles (for Fr.4.50), each uniquely colored (all the glass we'd seen being made ended up perfectly clear), and she took us back across the street, round the building, and into a small park with the world's largest and goofiest pinball machine imaginable. Here Irma gave us each three marbles and we climbed steep steps and rolled our marbles, one at a time, into the clever little wire gutters which guided our marbles till they dropped and spun and tinkled through a maze of wire and glass, making wonderful little glass tinkly sounds, until they each rolled out into a little basin below and to one side. We giggled like kindergarten pupils on a field trip, grabbed our marbles, and ran up the ladders to do it all over again.

It was dusk by the time we finally left, a few ducks and gulls bobbing languidly in the grey water of the lake. We were wonderfully lighthearted. Susanna and I thanked Irma profusely for this delightful adventure. Irma handed Susanna all the marbles to give, eventually, to Woody. And I can picture him there, as captivated by the glassworks as we were, pinball machine and all.

almost noon
Friday, February 2

Susanna's fixing lunch. Vater has gone to eat with Mama at the *Altersheim*.

Susanna's better—we're both *better*—but neither of us is *well*. It's incredible how this stuff drags on.

Between Vater and Susanna, the CD player in the music room was conjured to work this morning, and we listened to a Swiss production of Bertoni's opera "Orfeo". The CD was a gift to her parents from Julia, Susanna's oldest sister, who, in her fabulous alto voice, sings the lead role in this tearjerker of love that proves stronger even than death.

Is "Orfeo" an allegory on the resurrection of Jesus, of love that willingly faces death (but also overcomes death) rather than knuckle under to fear and self-preservation? Ah, the invisible love of God that sustains us all, just as we are sustained by the very air we breathe, about which we think nothing and take so utterly for granted.

Nature, art, and religion—these three timeless and inexhaustible themes. Here is Paustovsky on nature: "People usually go to nature as to a vacation. But I felt a life in nature should be the constant vocation of every man." Perhaps, as a writer, he could have said a similar thing about art. The monk Thomas Merton could certainly have said something like it about religion.

Wednesday evening, coming back through Lucerne from the glassworks, Irma asked how I liked the big Jesuit church, the one Susanna and I had ducked into briefly, next to the River Reuss, near the big wooden footbridges.

"I have contradictory feelings," I replied. "On the one hand, I am overpowered, thrown into sheer awe, by the massive architecture, by its symmetry, elegance, and workmanship. On the other hand, I am bewildered and dismayed, thrown into confusion, when I try to connect this artistic *thing*, this heap of self-satisfied vanity, to the wandering, dusty life of the very outdoors Jesus I read about in four small gospels."

"Ah, yes," replied Irma. "I too for its Baroque admire; but as *Kirche*, nozzings!"

So where is this extremely subtle, slippery line—which we all confront in our most ordinary daily lives—between emptying ourselves of vanity and puffing ourselves up? Between growth that comes by letting go of our pettiness and self-importance and the decay that hardens us as we build our shells of grandeur?

How we answer, how we respond to, this elemental problem shapes not only our individual lives, but our collective social and cultural lives, as well. This is why some theologians can talk not only about *personal* sin, but also about *collective* and *institutional* sin.

It is only in this way that it may be possible to ethically examine the doctrine and practice of "progress," our greedy consumption of natural resources, the wealth chasm between rich and poor countries, the cost of a health-care system which for an individual's sickness and old age begins to exceed the money a poor person can earn in a lifetime, the way we turn our back on the problem of long-term nuclear waste disposal, our resentful disinclination to keep alive handcrafts, low-energy agriculture, horses and buggies, low-energy *living*!

Art, too—decorative art, especially—too often turns its back on the lowly (except to make it picturesque and sweet and sentimental), just as the gorgeously-robed bishop glances with scorn and disapproval at the dusty feet of the humble monk, just as we snap one more photograph of the exquisite waterfall before jumping in our air-conditioned car, complete with sound system, and race to the next "foto-op."

The promise, and threat, of the Christian religion is that, someday, beyond the grave, we will each be called upon to account for who we are. And how will we each feel, in the expectant hush of those who wait to hear, when we know, when we know!, that nothing we can possibly say exonerates us from our puffy vanity and grim falsity; and we stand there, in the grip of a terrible, healing humiliation, tears streaming down our faces, sobbing, knowing that only the mercy of God can save us, and make us whole.

In God's mercy, nature and art and religion converge.

Friday evening

The colorful, old beggar woman (though Irma said she is not a beggar and that she responds with indignation if anyone approaches her as such) was sitting on the bench outside the *Polizeiwache*, the police station, where we caught the bus last Wednesday morning. When the bus left she sat there still, her heavy boots thrust out in front of her, her torso lying almost in her own lap, her head held sideways above her knees in a thick-fingered hand.

We had seen her twice before, both times in Lucerne, once in the basement of the *Bahnhof*. She invariably wore layer upon layer of heavy, dark clothing, looking like a medieval peasant out of a Breughel painting. She lives, Irma says, in a tiny trailer, in Irma's own suburb, and somehow she survives. The authorities don't know what to do with her, so they let her alone. She seemed like a relic, an icon almost, a demented oracle whose prophecies everyone would be terrified to hear, if ever she chose to utter them.

The bus arrived at the cold *Bahnhof* a good half hour before our train was scheduled to leave. Susanna had a sore throat, was cold, needed something to drink, and had to go to the bathroom. She fetched us each a can of soda (made with fruit juice) from a cafeteria with its name spelled out in blue neon letters, went to the women's bathroom, and came back angry.

Later, at the *Altersheim* in Sulgen, in the dining room where Mama and Vater were finishing their noon meal, Susanna told about the cans of juicy pop that cost Fr.3.20 each, and about the bathroom where, reluctantly, she was prepared to part with half a franc to use the toilet. But the toilet rental in the ultraviolet bathroom—ultraviolet, said Irma, so drug users can't see their veins—had gone up to a whole franc since the previous week. Susanna was indignant, stormed and fumed and laughed about the price of pee.

Later I told her Switzerland should put a sign at all its borders: *Achtung!* Attention! Poor People: Please Pee Before Entering!

This afternoon Susanna cleaned out the greenhouse, breaking the dry, brown stems of dead plants and putting the debris in the compost bin. We then went for a walk up the hill past the vineyard to where a small flock of sheep was grazing beneath bare apple trees. The sky was peculiar: dark, with light rain falling. But there was a rim of clear sky—as "clear" as Switzerland seems to get—way off to the south. And there, rising out of the haze, was the magnificent Säntis, the biggest mountain in northeastern Switzerland! *Wunderbar!*

Sunday morning
February 4

Es schneit! It's snowing, not a lot, but slowly and steadily. This *Wetter* (weather) has been so amazingly uniform that any little change is an occasion for notice and excitement. A real thunderstorm would be international news, if not also a virtual *Weltanschauung*.

Yesterday I asked Susanna a different sort of world view question: whether there are slums in Switzerland. She thought not. Certainly there are places in the bigger cities where most people wouldn't want to go at night, where it's dangerous, places where drug users hang out; but no slums, really.

And then I remembered this impression of a shanty town, as we were on the train from Lucerne to Zürich. I think it was northeast of Zug, just before the train dives through a couple tunnels and comes out near Horgen on the *Zürichsee*—Lake Zürich, I mean. What I saw was of course no shanty town at all, but only another community garden in which each tiny plot had its shed. Out of one of these brown sheds poked a small metal chimney with grey smoke drifting from it. The overall impression was of a deliberate *play* shanty town, a miniature enactment of cultural loss and nostalgia.

I somehow want there to be poor people here, and I suppose there are some (maybe mostly refugees, like the Yugoslav / Albanian immigrants), but they're certainly not conspicuous, nor are they likely to be the sort of poor people I have in mind.

What sort do I have in mind? I suppose this is my nostalgia, for I would love it if every society had a sizeable number of people—a cultural Amish, you might say—who declined most of the gadgets and conveniences of the twentieth century, whose daily lives provided a real and visible link with the pre-industrial past, so that we might have life as a historical continuum rather than as a technological chasm.

Vater asked me the other day (we three were having a discussion, over supper, on the new global economy) whether overproduction is a problem in America. Ah, I said, this is a tricky question, for it depends on the overproduction of *what*. On the basis that we radically undervalue fossil fuel, oil in particular, there is no doubt whatsoever that there is a massive worldwide overproduction of those cute little plastic toys we call automobiles. What we *underproduce*, I said, are trains, solar panels and wind generators, buggies with frictionless running gear for horses, doctors who make house calls (and whose incomes are modest), footpaths, and coffeehouses with live music. We underproduce our own furniture, homes, and handcrafts. We underproduce rural, decentralized elementary schools with vigorous teachers who take their students outside to look at bugs and bushes, swamp water and stars, who teach languages conversationally and a multitude of crafts.

I argued that this vision is *not* "utopian." My reason for doing so runs something like this. "Utopian" means an attempt to achieve a perfect system. Soviet communism was such an attempt at utopia, and so is technological capitalism. The thrust of Western thinking since the Enlightenment of the eighteenth century has been toward rational, scientific perfection. In this effort, many technological wonders (and horrors) have been achieved; but its philosophical base— the thrust toward perfection—is based on a false and finally wicked presumption. That presumption is that it's within human power, it's within the scope of the ethically permissible, to eat of the fruit of the Tree of Life: that we are capable of achieving the perfect, that the secret of life is available to us if we are ruthless enough to tear away its veils.

The great Revolution of modern times has been pointed in the wrong direction from the very beginning. It has wanted to "rise above" nature. It has exalted over the destruction of the peasantry and rural life. It has celebrated every possible "rise" in the Standard of Living. "The problem of the future is the use of leisure time!" Mechanization, electrification, computerization!

Embedded in practically all inventions is, perhaps, some small, practical, modest usefulness. With durable, carefully chosen goods; with a firm ethical determination to conserve natural resources and to minimize pollution; with the encouragement of cooperative land trust mini-villages blending agriculture and cottage industry; with limited and specific mass production—all this points to an entirely different society, culture, and political structure.

Under a broad ethical constitution, politics would be radically decentralized, thus ensuring the liveliness of local communities. And there would, of necessity, be structures of socialism for heavy infrastructure (railroads) and limited mass production (steel mills). But the question of ownership and public control is not the primary issue; and when it becomes the primary issue, as it did in the United States in the 1950s, something is radically wrong.

What was radically wrong in the 1950s? The headlong consumer stampede toward technological affluence, the cultural desiccation, all hid under, all justified by, the FEAR OF COMMUNISM. This was the theater of the great bogeyman—literally so in the personalities of Joe McCarthy and J. Edgar Hoover—impersonating the wrath of God. And now, instead of a human *culture* that is largely self-sustaining, we are burdened with layer upon layer of structural *organization*: industrial agribusiness, industrial health care, industrial entertainment, industrial education, etc., etc., etc.

Can this system last? And if, or when, it fails? When the system begins to break down, will we remember how to grow a potato, build a shed, knit a sock, sing a song, make a poem?

I told Vater I'd written a book once—*Nature's Unruly Mob: Farming and the Crisis in Rural Culture*—and at an earlier time it would've generated discussion and debate and maybe even earned me a modest livelihood. But by the time it was published in 1986, the issue was dead, intellectuals couldn't be bothered with the subject, the book was a joke.

Like the inscrutable face of "Kostik" Paustovsky which looked up at me last evening from the cover of his autobiography: water running into the tub, I'd stepped out into the hallway where Vater sat at a small wooden table, playing solitaire with a worn deck of tiny cards, cigar smoke rising in the lamplight, and had taken off my outer shirt, moccasins, and socks.

When I returned to the bathroom, I discovered I'd bumped Paustovsky. I found him floating face up in the tub, looking up at me as if to say, "You have all the brains of an empty dipstick in a dead horse, and the brilliance of a turtle's hind footprint." Drowning, I knew, would be of no avail. So I plucked him out, those big black eyes following me without a flinch or a flicker, and set him on his ear to dry.

That face stares up at me now, as if to say, "Vell, Meester *Amerikanisch* Bozo, velcome to da vorld oof modern leeturature. Hangg in der und goot luk!"

The problem is the underlying brokenness and poverty of everyday culture. Literature sings over this wreckage and amnesia a sobbing song of remembrance and hope. Without hope, there is no life. Without hope, Utopia turns to us its wicked skull face and laughs in our teeth.

Therefore we hope.

Tuesday morning
February 6

Susanna, more observant than I, noticed that the footprints we'd made in the thin snow, in the morning, had no additional snow in them when we'd returned, late yesterday afternoon. We'd left Sulgen at 11:14, sharp. Even with several stops (this was not a *Schnellzug*, a fast train), we arrived before noon in St. Gallen.

St. Gallen lies in a narrow valley, and opens like a hand-held fan to the northeast. We entered from the southwest, passing through Gossau with its big undulating hills that remind one of southern Wisconsin, and through Winkeln with its old castle perched on a hill (Susanna pointed it out to me through the train window) where she and her family would come for a Sunday afternoon when she was a child, where somebody she knew got married, in the big room above the torture chamber....

Snow fell the entire time we were in St. Gallen. For a while snow fell while the sun was shining, the snowflakes glinting and flashing in their languid descent like crystallized sunshine.

We almost didn't go, neither of us feeling well. But we finally decided we could stay at home and rot in snot, choke in smoke, or we could go out and act alive, even if it killed us. Vater drove us into Sulgen, he saw Mama, we slipped into the train like two fat slugs in a frosty garden.

It was a simply glorious day. *Wunderbar.*

The train stations in smaller towns like Sulgen are like the train stations I knew in small Wisconsin towns in my youth; that is, the boarding platform is outside, maybe with a roof but also maybe not. The big train stations in Zürich and Lucerne have twenty or more tracks, the whole terminal covered by a vast dome. So I wondered what the *Bahnhof* in St. Gallen would be like. It proved to be a smaller version of Zürich or Lucerne. And although it was just as cold, just as blue and grey, there were vendors selling sandwiches and fruit, kiosks with magazines and cards. The impression was of a greater liveliness, more relaxed, less business-driven.

Susanna took me first to the streets to the north of the station. Within five minutes, we were standing in front of the apartment building she lived in from 1951 to 1960. The same Seventh-Day

St. Gallen.

Adventist mission was on the ground floor of the building next door, exactly as it had been in her childhood.

We then went back through the *Bahnhof* and out on the streets to the southeast: and it was there, in the old city, where we walked and roamed throughout the afternoon, Susanna holding onto me by a long rope tied around my waist, my head revolving like a barber pole, my eyes pulsing and twitching. Susanna was the Irish monk Saint Gall and I was her shuffling Swiss bear. The year was 612 A.D. and Susanna was attempting to tug her *bärbeissig Flattergeist*, her bearish unsteady husband, through the woods.

Like in the old part of Lucerne, there is in St. Gallen an extensive area with narrow, crooked, cobblestone streets, with wonderfully ornamented balconies and bay windows jutting out. The buildings were old—several centuries old—mostly three and four stories high; and they were built tight together, with sometimes little archways opening in and through, but otherwise continuous. Motorized traffic was limited to pickup and delivery, so people walked everywhere and anywhere.

We went inside the huge old Catholic church, ornamented and elegant and ornate, but somehow less brassy, more modest and more serene than the in-your-face Jesuit church in Lucerne. We tried to get into the huge Protestant church nearby, but it was locked—which certainly

St. Gallen.

Intricate brasswork found in St. Gallen.

did nothing to dispel sociologist Max Weber's assertion that Calvinism is the religion of upwardly-striving suspicion.

And everywhere the doors! Church doors were, of course, fabulous with their carved woodwork and intricate iron hinges. But old St. Gallen is everywhere a city of fabulous doors, of extravagant hinges, of latches that are works of art.

We bought some *Fladen* (flat cakes) in a wonderful *Bäckerei* and walked down narrow streets, happily munching the delicious hot food. Susanna was taking me to Christoph Sprenger's violin shop and—life is, if not exactly full, then plump with these experiences—ran into her old Brienzer schoolmate exactly at the street entrance to his second-floor store and shop. Susanna introduced us, calling Christoph "a rich violin maker." Christoph, silver-haired, smallish, plump, and laughing, invited us up, saying Susanna still talks as foolishly as she did twenty-five years ago.

Up in the cluttered shop with ugly brown linoleum floor (which opened, by door, into a lovely little store with a wonderfully squeaky parquet floor) Susanna had to tell me again the story of how Christoph accidentally allowed Johannes Finkel's father's Volkswagen beetle to roll down a hill into a lake, and sink, headlights still shining, back in the good old days of violin makers' school. It seemed to me that Christoph actually blushed, as if he's still embarrassed by that escapade.

Susanna translating, there followed a discussion of the violin makers' school, of the vote taken by the established violin makers on whether or not to close the school. It never became clear whether Christoph was the only one to do so, but he voted to close, saying there are already too many violin makers. I couldn't help but raise

Susanna with Christoph Sprenger.

the example of Johannes Finkel, with his Fr.250,000 computerized machine to rough out violins, as the real problem. Christoph shrugged in resignation, saying "This sort of thing is going on all over the world, and with far more sophisticated equipment than Johannes has."

We stayed most of an hour. An employee of Christoph's came in, balding, with a little earring, sat down at the workbench and began to repair a bow. We had a little tour of the store and left.

By then we wanted a cup of coffee, so after walking for a while, Susanna took me into a little corner cafe. This was, probably, the third or fourth time since coming to Switzerland that I've been startled by the sound of country western music, direct from Nashville, tumbling out of ceiling speakers. "Shall we go?" Susanna asked. "No," I said, "the contrast is too exquisite." So we ordered and drank the delicious, expensive coffee, the tall, dark-haired, good-looking waitress coming to our window table with that same feeling of restless boredom one would virtually expect in a waitress in a cafe in a western Nebraska town.

So that too was a subtle lesson: boredom is where you find it, a state of mind, maybe a state of music, a condition of the spirit. Perhaps country western *is* the music of boredom.

Susanna said that if we were feeling better and if there was more time, she'd take me "up there," gesturing through the lacy window curtain up the hill. "That's where the cloister is, where as children we put our order and money in this little revolving door, and pretty soon a small bag of cookies would be turned out to us. We called them — everybody did—*Nonnefürzli*, little nunfarts. They were good."

We left (we had maybe an hour before our train would leave) and went on a hurried tour of the *Gymnasium*, theater, museum—by walking past; we didn't have time to go in—and a couple parks complete with huge beech trees and fountains. The snow just barely covered the grass. I thought we were going to a particular museum, for we'd looked without success (but with suggestions of where to look) for cards with art by Giovanni Segantini. Walking briskly through a park, I suddenly stopped and said, "If we ever live in St. Gallen, I want us to live in an apartment house just like that." I pointed at an old five-story, long, brick apartment building that reeked of solidity and modest comfort, with windows that looked directly into the park.

"Really?" asked Susanna, with a laugh of amazement. "That's exactly where I lived from 1960 until 1964!" It was my turn to be dumbfounded. We walked over, and I took a photograph of Susanna standing in her old doorway.

We had to hurry, and I was taken on a whirlwind tour of Susanna's old neighborhood—old apartment houses, old houses, the girls' high school where Susanna and her sisters had their secondary education. Students were pouring out as we walked by the old three-story grey building, both girls and boys, many of them dressed in blue jeans, a cluster of boys and girls gathered outside a main door busily lighting cigarettes, several of them with beginner's awkwardness.

I asked Susanna whether girls wore pants when she was in school. No, of course not, and no smoking either, none, zero, *absolutely* not.

Susanna pointed out the third-floor music room where Vater

taught choir for years, where he had made a shy girl, who later became a professional singer, go down to the lawn and sing loudly enough for him to hear, standing near an open window in the music room.

From there Susanna hunted for and, with the help of an elderly woman on the street, found an old cloister (not used as a cloister since the time of the Reformation) called St. Katharinen. This marvelous place was tucked behind a perfectly inconspicuous door which opened onto a rectangular, arched walkway with large brick-colored tiles on the floor, surrounding a tiny rectangular garden, open to the sky, with a crossed walkway through it. Susanna was thrilled to find it, to share it, rather like the children in Frances Hodgson Burnett's book, *The Secret Garden*.

Then it was time to walk hurriedly to the *Bahnhof*, happy as schoolkids on a Friday afternoon. We found our *Zug*, got on, and waited. The train alongside began to move and I experienced all over again that strange vertigo which occurs when you feel you're

Susanna in St. Katharinen.

moving but you're not. As always, it passed quickly.

Once the train started to roll, we were soon out of St. Gallen. I waited expectantly for a view of the long, high, arched bridges we'd glimpsed coming in. After that, we ate oranges and chatted cheerfully all the way back to Sulgen.

We went to see Mama, busy with the *Altersheim* physical therapist when we walked into her room. The therapist left, supper was brought in on a tray for Mama, Vater arrived wearing his beaver hat. We chatted about St. Gallen, Mama ate, and then we left—Vater, Susanna, and I.

On our way home, Vater stopped at the kiosk by the *Bahnhof* to buy some "ammunition"—cigars—and returned with a copy of the INTERNATIONAL HERALD TRIBUNE for me. Its headlines read: U.S. DEMANDS THAT BELGRADE HELP EXTRADITE BOSNIAN SERBS; EU HEADING FOR POLITICAL CRISIS, KOHL AIDE SAYS; YELTSIN AGAIN MAKES COSTLY PROMISES, THIS TIME TO MINERS; DRASTIC PERSONNEL CUTS EXPECTED AT UN; DRESS CODE: JIANG'S CLOTHES REFLECT HIS POLITICAL THINKING; WINTER DEALS U.S. ANOTHER ICY BLOW. And, in a side bar with tiny map, there was a mini-report of an earthquake in China that killed 240 people, injured "about" 14,000 people, that registered 7.0 on the Richter scale.

My little day had been spent comfortably sight-seeing, with the sniffles, blowing my nose, all too inconspicuous to register on anybody's Richter scale. Achoo! *und Gesundheit.*

late Tuesday afternoon

Margrit Lässker, our only neighbor up the hill, right behind our back yard, invited Vater and Susanna and me to dinner today—the noon meal. We arrived promptly and were ushered with great cheerfulness up the dark, heavy stairway, with two turns in it, to the living room with its northeast corner given over to the dining room table. The living room is part of the new house: the old part, with heavy beams very much intact, complete with cobwebs, was a building for the pressing of grapes. But the new part was built to harmonize with the old: a floor of brick-colored tiles, each a foot square, with a broad band of grey grout between; walls of rough white stucco; a ceiling of beams and unpainted lumber.

In one corner stood an old blonde upright piano, with music open on the stand. Two identical brown easy chairs, worn but quite serviceable, stood on a Persian rug, eight feet by twelve, along with an oak coffee table with a tile top, and a simple curved couch. Against the east wall was a fireplace with a raised hearth; a small fire was glowing there, with orange coals, behind a sliding screen.

Dinner consisted, first, of cabbage salad and beet salad; second, of boiled potatoes and *Raclette*— hot, melted cheese. Susanna and I sat on one side of the table, Vater and Margrit (almost exactly the same age) on the other. On the basis of a few months in England as a governess many, many years ago— she was almost caught there by the outbreak of World War II— Margrit speaks a limited but remarkably lucid English. There she sat, a small, bouncy woman with steel-grey hair swept back from her firm, strong face, wearing an elbow-length black wool sweater over a white blouse with its

Margrit Lässker.

collar turned out, watching everything and everybody with great intensity through thick, yellowish glasses. We were all perfectly at ease, and perfectly mannerly.

The food was delicious (a tiny glass of cherry brandy each for Vater and me after the meal), including Margrit's own frozen strawberries—*Erdbeeren*, earthberries, in German—topped with whipped cream, for dessert. Shortly after, Vater excused himself to go take his eyedrops—and a nap. Susanna and I stayed on. Margrit brought out coffee, the typical wonderful Swiss coffee, and a homemade pearbread, which was really a long, rolled pastry made with dried pears in a flaky crust.

Susanna explained to me that pearbread is a food common to all of Switzerland, but that each region prepares it differently. Margrit's pearbread is a Graubünden recipe: that canton in southeastern Switzerland that borders Liechtenstein, Austria, and Italy. It is from this canton, and furthermore that part of the canton north of Chur which is "Heidi country," that Margrit originates.

Margrit told stories of her late husband, who was thirty-nine years her senior, who designed the Buchenberg (Margrit and her husband lived here, long before Vater and Mama bought it), and who was largely an untaught mechanical genius, an inventor. A toy car he made, displayed in a Paris show, won him unanticipated lifelong employment as a designer for a large Swiss industrial concern. At the age of nineteen, he made a toy cannon with which he shot chickens—until the *Polizei* came and confiscated it.

For a while Margrit and Susanna talked wistfully of Graubünden, for the Juons also originate from that canton—if any of us can be said to "originate" anywhere. They talked of Romansh, that odd, old language peculiar to Switzerland and to Graubünden. Margrit said it was maybe brought to Switzerland long ago by Romanian gypsies. No, said Susanna (there are also suggestions of Gypsy blood among the Juons), the Gypsy language has been traced all the way back to India.

"Ah," said Margrit, her eyes flashing, "how I loved the big Gypsy tent when I was a child! I told my father, 'I want to go with the Gypsies!' 'Go,' he said. But I didn't. I even loved the Salvation Army, when they would come through with their guitars, and sing, and ask for money!"

"Ah," she said, "everything has come too far, too fast. We need to go backwards a little, you know what I mean?" We agreed that, here and there, there are a few people who choose, with little or no support, to "go backwards a little," and that this tendency could grow if only governments would encourage it.

I was reminded of a story in yesterday's newspaper, a feature piece by Michael Specter, on the Tambov region about three hundred miles southeast of Moscow, in Russia. This is, according to Specter, a fertile farming area, a region that defied Soviet attempts from 1918 to 1921 to confiscate food and that now defies the so-called reformers by electing a majority of communists to local governing bodies, sending a communist delegate to the parliament, and flying the red flag over city hall.

My hunch is that Russia, and perhaps a number of Eastern European countries, will move in fits and starts back to socialism. But I think this will be a far gentler socialism—a socialism concerned with democracy, cultural stability, and the quality of life—than the previous Soviet system with its "scientific materialism." This new socialism will be a far greater "threat" to the West (if the West chooses to see it as a threat) than the former system. Why? Because its appeal will be less ideological and more ethical; it won't be hysterically atheist, for one thing. Plus life in the West will become poorer, more difficult; its arrogant individualism will wear itself threadbare. The new Russian bear might prove to be a very gentle dancer from whom the West might learn a step or two.

In the meantime, the most promising direction is "backwards a little, you know what I mean?"

Wednesday morning
February 7

Es schneit, slowly and lightly. Done with dishes. Vater's gone to run some errands and to bring Mama home for dinner and for the afternoon. Susanna's cooking a chicken soup.

Every few days I give Susanna my journal to read. I did so last night, before we went to bed. As a rule, she enjoys the descriptions, laughs at my jokes and clownish exaggerations, but "sometimes cringes" at my harshness. Here lies a hub of my uncertainty.

There are times when I agree totally with this "cringing," when I am disturbed by my own writing. And these harsh words probably are to some immeasurable extent an expression of my inability to say the same thing with gentleness—an emotional failing, in other words, a tendency toward arid preachiness. And yet....

Our conversation in the kitchen moved in and out of the topic of religion: how churches are the repository of excellence in artistic expression, each according to its own ideas, taste, and self-imposed limitations; how great artists and craftsmen of past centuries worked either for the aristocracy or for the church, for that's where the loot was, the capital, the bread and sausage and a place to sleep. Yet Jesus pointed out the old woman, who, with her two pennies, gave more than all the rest—because she gave all, while the others gave only out of their abundance. Or the constant reminders in the Bible that what God wants from us is not our deep-pocket patronage or great artistic achievement, but our broken hearts, our genuine repentance, our self-emptying.

And so the life of Jesus, as portrayed in the four gospels, is full of conflict, of accusation and harshness, this Jesus who sits like a perpetual thorn under the ornate saddle of civilization, this Jesus who goads us constantly with his totally empty, self-sacrificial life, who cleanly and boldly and with hardly a wisp of hesitation shows us a narrow, winding, rocky pathway, beckons us to follow—and we all stand uncertainly, gnawing on the sides of our mouths, thinking of all the things we'd rather be doing, fun things, more relaxing things, things with a future we can plan.

I don't mean to say that my harshness qualifies me as a little Jesus. I'm not a little Jesus. I'm a *Nebelpumpe*, a little *amerikanisch* twirp, *der Kaiser Rotbart*: but I also do mean what I say—allowances given for blatant lies, lumberjack tall tales, and pinch-lipped preachiness.

Forgive me, dear reader, for the poor pulpit splintered by excessive pounding. But, I beg you to hear the plaintive little melody in all this bombastical ranting and raving. Sweet melody *mit* foghorn.

late Wednesday afternoon

Susanna and I wrote postcards to friends in America, then walked to Heldswil, just south of Götighofen, to mail them. Susanna came back to be with Mama; but I walked west on a road I'd not been on before, toward Kradolf and the Thur River.

At first the road went fairly straight between small fields. But then it made a bend into a completely wooded area. Here, on the left side of the road, built between and partly hidden by two towering spruce, was a simple bench made of boards, painted red, with one end crudely chopped, as if with a hatchet, to fit the curve of a root. I wiped snow off the bench and sat for a long time, the woods going up behind me, the narrow road in front. On the other side of the road, a ravine fell sharply, wooded with spruce and beech, some of the spruce rising easily eighty or one hundred feet into the air.

At the bottom of the ravine there was the constant small splash of an icy brook I could not see. Then the other wooded bank of the ravine rose up, behind which was an upsloping meadow crowned with woods. From that meadow came a sweet tinkling like wind chimes, which I knew to be the tiny bells of sheep.

It was cool, but the sun was shining warmly enough to melt the thin snow in the meadow. I sat there in my wool coat, enjoying the scene and the sounds, soaking in the peacefulness, thinking about Vater's answer to my question of how the church would have to change for him to want to attend more regularly (a "more artistic service," was his reply), thinking of those people for whom this very scene of snowy woods and gurgling water and tinkly bells could be their "cathedral"—or, rather, the red wooden bench, for the word derives from the Latin *cathedra*, meaning bishop's chair. And I thought, too, of old Doc Sievert, a dentist of the old school from my hometown, who owned land and built a cottage right along the Newood River, a good mile upstream from the farm I grew up on.

Doc had a footbridge across the river. He had little grassy roads that twisted and turned, not only along the river, but through the woods, around swamps and hills. And he had little benches here and there, at especially scenic points, and birdhouses, and discard cemetery monuments carved with little poems and aphorisms, a bust of Beethoven.

I distrust religion that has no true reverence for nature, for how can a person who is merely utilitarian about Creation claim to revere the Creator? There are those—and I think Vater is more or less in esthetic league with them—who find their own cathedral (Vater's features the music of Johann Sebastian Bach rather prominently) because the formal church is so arid, pompous, self-important, theatrical, bombastic, and just plain boring.

Old Doc with his safari hat and mosquito veil, and Vater with his bushy eyebrows and grand piano, would have had a lot in common. At least their *Weltanschauungen*, their world views, would have strongly overlapped—thoughtful humanists, lovers of artistic beauty and natural beauty, philosophical ponderers. This is *culture* at its richest and most humane. The church, as it now exists, tends to be a pretty inadequate pot, dry and pinched, for these bushy, vigorous plants to grow in. The church would squint down its long, narrow nose at them, and reach for its prim little electric hedge clipper.

But Jesus—I think—might walk right by the parsonage, with its blue bug zapper, and sit down in a tumble of Bach fugues, in a little cottage by the river, and enjoy not only a meal of fresh fish but also a truly openhearted conversation, with the gurgling music of dark water trickling in through the windows.

So I believe.

Wednesday night

After supper, Vater took Mama back to the *Altersheim*. Susanna and I washed dishes, played music, and now Susanna's on the phone with the Juons' old family friend Frau Doktor Annemarie Frick, who's calling from St. Gallen.

There are a couple of things relating to money I want to slip in.

Milk comes in one liter containers. Four liters in a package cost Fr.7.40. In U.S. terms, milk would cost over $6.00 per gallon. Two hundred grams of butter cost Fr.3.10. This would be over $6.00 per pound. However (tenuous as a single example is) Susanna learned today that the woman who comes here to clean with her *Staubsauger* ("dustsucker") one afternoon per week—a cheerful redhead who is a nonstop talker in her thirties—will soon begin to work as an aide in a nursing home for a starting wage of Fr.20.00 per hour. A new aide in a nursing home in our area of Wisconsin would start at maybe $5.25 per hour. So, while prices are high, wages are high too. This gives the unmistakable impression of a self-enclosed economy which enjoys a high standard of living, including its agricultural "sector." Hence the great misgivings in Switzerland—Vater fairly squirms with these misgivings—about Switzerland joining, and being over-whelmed by, the European Union.

When we stopped for "ammunition" and a newspaper Monday evening at the kiosk near the *Bahnhof,* I paid closer attention to a sign I'd seen before. It read: "TOTO LOTTO LOSE". I asked Susanna what it meant, and she explained that it's an advertisement for the Swiss lottery that's been operating for years.

Vater later explained that "TOTO" refers to a soccer lottery, "LOTTO" means lottery, and "LOSE" ("low-za") is a ticket you might win something with.

Through Susanna I conveyed to him the *amerikanisch* meaning of *LOT TO LOSE,* which he thought extremely funny in a wicked sort of way. Which is sort of like, but not exactly like, Switzerland's chancy future in the political rugby of European Union. TOTO LOTTO LOSE.

A ticket to win? Or a whole lot to lose?

Thursday afternoon, late
February 8

At the moment of the 1917 Russian Revolution, Kostik Paustovsky says, the intellectuals—the "intelligentsia"—mostly lost their heads. They had known how to create "high spiritual values," but they proved worthless and helpless at "creating the organization of a state." But is this really a mystery?

Ultimately, the church rests on the principle of mercy, while the state is built on the principle of order. In the long run, mercy always outlasts order: the Roman Empire died—first the Western and then the Eastern arm—but Christianity lives on. Tolstoy outlives Stalin.

The intelligentsia live largely in the cultural space between these two—between order and mercy, between the state and religion. In the Christian perspective, nothing exceeds, nothing greater follows, the stupendous example of the mercy of Christ nailed to the cross. Everything and everybody that follows is but a footnote, perhaps a minor variation, of this ultimate mercy.

The state, meanwhile, has a number of models from which to choose for its conception and practice of order; but it has no ultimate model. One could say there have been attempts at, or presumptions of, an ultimate model: the Egyptian dynasties, the Chinese empires, the Greek city-state, the Roman Republic, the Aztec theocracy, American democratic capitalism, Soviet communism, Hitler's Third Reich. What they have in common is that degree of amassed capital and organized class we call civilization, and a propensity to impose a certain kind of brutal order on those "below."

Order has typically been imposed by a wealthy, strong, and even ruthless ruling class. The history of civilization is very largely the study of how, and in what way, any particular ruling class conducted itself—how warlike it may have been, what its artistic tastes were—at any particular place and time. There is seldom any mercy to be found in any of this, for mercy is a weakness to order. Order, if pressed hard enough by popular demand, may compromise in the direction of justice, the rule of law applied "blindly."

Order is hard, shortsighted, and lives in the head. Mercy is soft, farsighted, and lives in the heart. When order rejects mercy absolutely, it lives totally in its "scientific" head and cannot help but become deranged and despotic. One of the major tasks of mercy is to be forever calling order to task for its blindness, excesses, and lapses.

But because these contending principles are made up of real

people, with all the oddities, impulses, delusions, and generous tendencies common to our human race, things get muddled as a matter of course. People who believe themselves on the mercy side of things can shout themselves hoarse about the necessity of imposing God's will. This can be a big problem, for not only does it confuse order with mercy, it also makes mercy a laughingstock to those hard-boiled types whose passion it is to plan for order. (Order has been known to cheerfully posture itself in purple robes, smirking all the while.)

The task of the intelligentsia, in other words, is still to espouse "high spiritual values." It is and always will be. But one must beware of condemning the intelligentsia too much for its powerlessness, for its paralysis, at the occasion of the Russian Revolution. An utterly rotten system (*serfdom* had only been abolished in Russia in the 1860s) was collapsing from within and from without. Looking back it seems inevitable that a ruthless new authoritarianism would rise from that colossal historic wreckage. And it did.

So—what now for this great, fantastical Russian country, with its seething literary and artistic heritage that the great writer Konstantin Paustovsky loves so deeply?

Let mercy be our guide. Let the Russian people slowly choose their new order, for this is not a decision to be reversed in a day, or a year, or a lifetime. And let the West keep its market-greedy fingers out of the Russian pie. Fast food is not the ultimate in spiritual values. The long-term peace and health and prosperity of a people depend on the depth and richness and stability of their *culture*. This requires that we get out of our heads and start seeing from our hearts.

Saturday morning
February 10

We got up late, and I was just sitting down to the breakfast table—Vater had already eaten and was playing a solitary game with his tiny cards at the wooden table in the second-floor hallway, the entire scene wreathed in blue-grey wisps of cigar smoke—when

Susanna said, "Aren't you at least going to say hello?"

Puzzled, but thinking it was perhaps an unusual bird, I got up and walked to the south window, where she was standing, looking out. And there, as if the road through Götighofen were a gun barrel, stood the Säntis like a majestic front sight, rising proudly above the haze!

Annemarie, in consultation with an unknown *Wetterprophet*, had called it exactly right. In her phone conversation with Susanna Wednesday night, she had said she wanted to take us to the Säntis and Friday would be the only day this week the sky would clear. "We've got to grab it," she said.

On Thursday morning we woke to the heaviest snowfall yet. By Thursday afternoon the snowplows and sand trucks were out. Susanna and I took a two-hour, looping, snow-shuffling walk to Kradolf and back. In a small patch of woods, an old woman, bent over and bundled up, met us on the narrow gravel road. It was snowing heavily. There was no traffic. We were coming out of the woods; she was coming in. We were all covered—even our eyebrows—with a mantle of snow. In response to our greeting, she looked at us with what I can only call a happy solemnity, returned our greeting, and, looking into the woods, said softly, "*So schön!*" (So beautiful!) On her old face was a look of undisguised reverence and joy.

Friday morning the sun was shining brilliantly on the thick white snow, as Susanna and I walked into Sulgen. We visited briefly with Mama, then caught the 8:14 *Zug* to Gossau. The landscape all the way was brilliant, clean, and white. Annemarie met us precisely at the edge of the *Bahnhof* parking lot—met us with great warmth and eagerness—and we piled into her little red Nissan.

She drove us immediately out of Gossau toward Wil, which lies to the northwest. As the Säntis lies—or, as I should say, *towers*—to the south and slightly to the east of Gossau, I was at first confused by this route. Annemarie explained that the big highway would be pretty clean and a lot less dangerous than the smaller, snow-covered roads. Even so, as we drove Annemarie had to repeatedly wash the *Windschutzscheibe*, the windshield, to get rid of the slush thrown up by other vehicles, slush that quickly dried to a *nebel*like opaqueness.

From the outskirts of Wil, we turned southeast, more or less following the Thur River upstream. We went through Bütschwil, Lichtensteig, and Wattwil. With each successive town the landscape grew wilder, more rugged, the snow deeper. We were entering that mountainous region called the Toggenburg. The older houses, with their flared eaves, began to have what Annemarie called "that peculiar Toggenburg characteristic."

The road drifted slightly more east through Ebnat-Kappel and Krummenau. By Nesslau, Annemarie took a hard left, and we began to climb in earnest, upstream along a little tributary of the Thur, through Rietbad to Schwägalp, at the very northwestern foot of the Säntis. On the way from Wil, we had passed a covered, single-lane wooden bridge, built with massive timbers and brown with age. We had zoomed on by at least two very high arched bridges made of stone. We had zipped past innumerable mountain scenes, enough to have given *Schlagfluss*, apoplexy, to any respectable photographer. (I thought of my good friend Mister Robert "Photopoint" Seitz, holed up in his fifty-below cabin in northern Wisconsin.) The little Thur tributary was practically buried under sugary snow, the banks overhung with snow-burdened boughs of massive spruce, dark water flowing between and around rocks heaped with snow muffins—the entire scene fresh, undisturbed, exquisite.

And we parked right at the foot of the Säntis, in ugly little Schwägalp, with its big, dumpy, boring tourist buildings, and its super-ugly cable car depot with its bright red and bright blue cable cars that go, on the half-hour, to the very summit of the Säntis.

In the depot there was a large glass display case with several stuffed animals: a *Steinbock* with huge, black, backsweeping, serrated horns; a *Gemse*, a much smaller mountain goat with single, backward-curving, antelope-sized horns; a big and little *Murmeltier*, furry woodchuck-sized critters; a *Schneehase*, a snow bunny, that looks less like our snowshoe hare and more like a prairie jackrabbit; and finally an *Alpendohle*, a small crowlike bird with orangeish-red legs and feet and an extremely bright yellow beak.

Susanna comes up to say it's time to go. Our social life is suddenly picking up steam, as it were. We're going to Weinfelden to see Tante Elsbeth, Susanna's aunt and Vater's next older sister. The weather is grey, as usual....

Sunday morning
February 11

Cloudy. No new *Schnee*. No filmy *Nebel*. Just normally *wolkig*, cloudy. Cloudy, cloudy, cloudy.

After breakfast, Susanna walked into Sulgen to go to church. Vater and I washed dishes. He managed to convey to me two things. First, the neighbors who've invited the three of us to the noon meal today both speak English. Second, he and I, because of the language difficulties, communicate through and with our eyes.

Now Vater takes eyedrops regularly—except, that is, when he forgets. So this morning his eyes were puffy, red, and watery. (I don't suppose the clouds of *Zigarre* smoke exactly help a lot.) But I so wanted to say what a sorry impression I must make on him, for when we communicate through and with our eyes, his get red and puffy and fill with tears!

This was one of life's true trials, when I wanted to play the clown (in Vater's idiom this would be called "making the calf"—*s' Chalb mache*) but couldn't.....

Well, yesterday I left us gazing with glazed eyes at a bunch of stuffed animals, while outside the cable car depot were two huge Swiss army trucks—olive *brown* I'd have to say, not olive green— with chains on all four wheels. The truckbeds were wrapped rather like old-fashioned covered wagons from the American pioneer days. And inside, on two long benches that faced each other, sat an unknown number of soldiers, dressed in dark camouflage, singing and yodeling in harmony.

After witnessing that wonderful military audition, we stepped into a blue cable car. The operator had a key to lock the sliding doors and a panel of buttons to push. He was dressed in dark blue pants and coat, had dark hair and a strong, open, utterly trustworthy workingman's face. He closed the doors, locked them, pocketed the key, punched a button—and off we went.

There were maybe a dozen people aboard. There were no benches. We all had to stand, though there were grips on the walls to hold onto. On the floor, on a pallet, was a dented, dirty, rusty backhoe bucket with freshly-welded teeth, the steel head of an industrial dinosaur. We gawked out the wraparound windows as we rose at an incredibly steep angle and at a surprisingly fast rate of speed. The earth fell away from us and became quickly toylike, a fairyland of play houses and cute little snow-dusted forests with tiny ribbons of dark road cunningly laid out in the doll world. Out of little speakers came accordion music and mountain singing, complete with yodeling. The experience was simultaneously awesome and a parody of itself. As Vater might say, *Phantastisch!*

The cable car slowed, bumped ever so little against the entrance guides, and stopped at the platform of the depot at the *top* of the Säntis. We went into this ugly cement building with the sliding glass doors (the cable car operator went to get a trolley hoist, jacked up the pallet with the backhoe bucket on it, and pulled it inside the building) and up a series of cement stairways, and then outside to a viewing platform that faced west. Here were people with cameras and binoculars. Overhead and (what else can I say?) *under*head swooped a whole disorderly gang of *Alpendohlen* with bright yellow beaks, orange feet, and feathers as black as midnight, all of them looking for tourists with dough, preferably baked.

Here we stood and gawked until Annemarie began to get chilled. We were, after all, standing on a mountain 2,500 meters above sea level, in the month of February, sunshine and sunglasses notwithstanding.

Annemarie took us into the restaurant and fed us—Saint Annemarie who *gave* us this day. As we ate (the food was good) the entire building trembled from the construction work going on behind concrete walls. We lingered over coffee and then went up to the very top outdoor observation platform, this one oriented to the southeast.

I have hesitated even to attempt to describe this incredible scene. We were standing, literally, on top of the world, the raw, jagged, violent, inhospitable teeth of gigantic rocks glaring up at the cold blue sky in utter disdain. Mountain after mountain sprawled away

View from the Säntis.

west and south and southeast. We were seeing mountains (Annemarie pointed them out, one by one) all the way to the Italian border. We gazed *over* Liechtenstein—we could see it, gauzy, on the east bank of the Rhine—into Austria, fold upon fold upon jagged fold of raw mountains disappearing beyond sight. It was as if we were viewing a massive boneyard of jaws and teeth from a multitude of prehistoric monsters too huge, too savage, too terrifying even to dream about. It was an *Alptraum*, a nightmare, literally so, *Phantastisch* and *Wunderbar*. Awesome.

I was reminded of the scene out the window of our jetliner as we flew over the west coast of France: this strange and humbling sense of awe at being in the realm of non-human forces, at seeing the earth, the habitable *Earth!*, so far below, beneath the wispy clouds, little clusters of pinpricks that were villages, towns, and even cities.

Annemarie pointed out pinprick St. Gallen, almost due north. We could see the hazy southeastern end of the blue-black Bodensee—and once there was a prolonged flash of light from it. I presumed a large boat was momentarily positioned just so, so that we were seeing sunlight reflected from its window. And I thought: not so long ago, this was as high as any human being could get; and the person who achieved this vantage point had to be strong and fit and brave to do it, a view that came only with risk and hard effort.

For us it was easy, almost effortless. Annemarie—this wonderful, generous person—rolled out the red carpet for us. The technical apparatus was in place, competent and ugly. But I couldn't rid myself of the feeling that I didn't earn this experience, that I took no risks to achieve it, that it came too easily. And yet I was, and am, in awe of what was there. This fantastic world! This incredible, sublime, terrifying world!

At 4:30—16:30 exact—we got back in the blue cable car with the reassuringly competent man in the blue pants and coat, and descended back to earth—down, down, down alongside the lean, raw flanks of grey stone. We thanked this man (everybody did who left the car) and he returned our words politely and modestly, this gentle conductor to the *Oberwelt*, the upper world.

Back in Annemarie's little red car, we headed down through Rietbad to Nesslau. At Susanna's wistful hint, we turned left not right, and went to Stein. Annemarie pulled off the road into a parking area (the snow was everywhere knee-deep) and Susanna, with longing in her voice, pointed out her parents' "weekend house"— this old combination farmhouse and barn perched on a very steep hillside that rises, rises, rises into a mountain to the south. (The road we were on—Swiss highways do not have numbers like American highways—fell, between mountains, to the east, through and past Wildhaus, Zwingli's hometown, all the way to the Rhine valley and, if one chose to cross the Rhine, to Liechtenstein—a mere twenty kilometers away.)

Annemarie took her little car, with its five-speed transmission, right up the crooked, winding one-lane road—plowed but, as we would say in Wisconsin, "snow-covered and slippery." We wiggled past little farms; but this time it was Susanna who was the *amerikanisch* pie face in *der Schweiz*, with her nose pressed flat against the little Nissan's foggy window. The road ended, *kaputt*, in the farmyard immediately above the weekend house. We didn't go down

The "weekend" house in Stein, as seen from the highway.

to it—no *Schlüssel*, no key, for one thing; plus the snow was several magnitudes deeper than Susanna's ankle-high shoes.

So Susanna stood and sighed and then, late afternoon duskiness beginning to settle in, we wiggled our way back down to Stein, right past an elderly farm woman standing next to a huge billy goat, both of them peering at us over a grey wooden fence as we drove by. At Stein, Annemarie turned left and took us, in the darkness, back to Wil.

We talked mostly of religion, Christianity old and new, the condition of the contemporary church. (Annemarie's father was a clergyman.) We all agreed the contemporary church has grown pretty anemic, suffocating in the sweet cushions of material comfort; that in the infinite lifestyle options of the Information Age, "sin" and "God's Judgment" are prehistoric linguistic relics. For the time being. While the "free market" lasts. While we're high on cheap oil and radioactive electricity and Japanese cars.

Annemarie took us in and through Wil, pointing out the hospital where she worked for nearly twenty years, and taking us quickly through old Wil, oval like an eye—beautiful even in the dark: half-timber and stucco and stone buildings tight together, a very narrow cobblestone street.

From Wil we returned to Götighofen via Bürglen and Sulgen. Annemarie asked us to run through the bewildering smorgasbord of Christian denominations in the United States. We agreed that it's a little peculiar for people to kill and slander one another over contending interpretations of the Golden Rule.

Our very own Saint Annemarie came in and had supper with us (Vater had just finished eating, but he sat with us), and then she left in an avalanche of our gratitude.

We went to bed with eyes feeling raw and dry from the glary sunlight on the Säntis, and from the wind. The Säntis! Monster teeth of geological amplitude! Jaws that drool glaciers! Sweet little Switzerland with its arcadian music and pretty girls in colorful skirts with hand-embroidered flowers! *Phantastisch!*

Sunday evening

As we say in the U.S., the faster I go the behinder I get.

We've been to dinner—roast ham *inside* a giant loaf of freshly baked bread, plus salad, two kinds of wine, a freshly-made sherbet with frozen berries whipped in a blender with cream, espresso coffee, and pound cake.

It is the Swiss tradition to bring gifts when invited to a meal. When we went to eat with Margrit Lässker, Vater bought a big fistful of tulips—which he made me carry and present. Today, he said, the gift would be the music Susanna and I would play and sing.

So at noon, exactly, lugging out instruments, we walked across the street to our nearest neighbors—well, maybe Margrit is closer—and were ushered graciously into this big house that's maybe six or seven years old. Black tile floor and fireplace, white stucco walls, beam and lumber ceiling—but all more modern and less cozy than Margrit's little vineyard hideout—lots of big windows with a wonderful view to the west, down the valley toward Sulgen and beyond.

Our hosts were Peter and Zita Forrer and their youngest daughter Fabienne, age seven. (The older daughter was gone with a group, skiing.) He teaches French to high school students. She works in a pharmacy. They travel often, have been to Disneyland and Yellowstone and the Grand Canyon, like American prices much better than Swiss prices, and believe Swiss waiters and waitresses are rivaled in rudeness and indifference only by Russian waiters and waitresses. (A first-class train from Moscow to Leningrad, in 1984, turned out to have no bathroom, no open windows, and only narrow wooden benches to sleep on.)

A little wine goes a long way with me. With two kinds of wine, I go a long way even faster. By the time Susanna and I played our music, my fingers had begun to tune into some unique frequency of tangled chords. I had to bring my internal schoolmaster into the scene, so to speak, to walk softly and carry a big metronome. (In my mind's eye, this schoolmaster was quite a hulking fellow, and his metronome resembled a cudgel carried by Little John, from the tales of Robin Hood.) We carried out our part rather well, actually; but I was ready to break into a serious sweat. I got up and stepped on my glasses....

In the end, as we left, I said, "If ever you vacation in the Great Lakes country, get our address from Vater and come see us." The thing is—I meant it.

later

Yes, one more social event to describe: our visit yesterday afternoon and evening with Tante Elsbeth and Vetter Walter. (*Tante* is aunt; *Vetter* is cousin.) Tante Elsbeth's late husband was Walter, too— and a brother to little Tante Emma Hut ("Hoot") who lives in the same *Altersheim* as Mama, in Sulgen.

Tante Elsbeth has an old, cheap, but not bad-sounding guitar hanging on her wall, in her third-floor apartment in Weinfelden. (Vater drove us there but did not come in.) Susanna had me tune the guitar—the tuning gears creaked and groaned like chiropractic exercises in a cemetery—so we could sing together that *wahnsinnig amerikanisch* song about Uncle Walter dancing with bears. Which was funny, cute and clever, but not nearly so fine as the old Swiss songs Susanna and Tante Elsbeth then sang in harmony.

Tante Elsbeth is eighty years old, short and wide, and she walks with her knees slightly bent and her torso tipped forward at a truly dangerous angle. (One's impulse is to help her with simply everything, which is probably exactly wrong.) Her face, with or without glasses, is strong—but softer without. Her skin is soft but full of wrin-

Tante Elsbeth.

kles, the patterns of which shift with her feelings and thought. Wrinkles around her eyes, wrinkles at the edges of her mouth, a forehead rippled with outlandish wrinkles that go crossways and up-and-down and meet high between her eyes in a veritable pucker of doubt or puzzlement or amusement, wrinkles of a keen intelligence.

While we ate—and we *had* to do this immediately upon arriving—she told us of marrying Walter, the farmer, when she was already thirty-eight; how she worked like a man (Tante Emma Hut, you see, Walter's sister, became the *Hausfrau*); how she and Walter, with a crosscut saw, cut logs on a steep hillside for four winters in order to have enough lumber to build a new barn. (Parts of the old barn were two centuries old, but they didn't tear it down because it was old. One of their cows had tuberculosis, and they were compelled to rid the barn of the disease in the most vigorous way.) She told us how she became a vegetarian in her childhood—her older sister's revulsion over the slaughter of a pig gradually changed the eating habits of the entire family—but how she loved the farm, loved the animals, the chickens especially.

They had an old-fashioned bakeoven on the farm in which a wood fire was built. When the oven was hot enough, the coals were scraped out, the oven given a quick wipe with a wet rag on a stick, and the bread (as many as fourteen loaves) pushed in.

In the midst of this conversation, Elsbeth's middle child, Walter Jr., arrived. He blew in pudgy and happy-go-lucky, with a serious five o'clock shadow, balding with thin, dark hair combed forward to cover his baldness. Walter ("Valter") speaks pretty good English, *hates* farming—"Vork, vork, vork, nozzings but vork. Eets not a life, eez only *vork*!"—but beneath his sharp words there is, I think, not only a farmer's quick mind but also a love for the land. Neither he

Walter and Tante Elsbeth.

nor his mother had a favorable thing to say about the European Union, and very little favorable to say about G.A.T.T. (General Agreement on Tariffs and Trade). All either can foresee is a depression of food prices at the farm level via cheap imports and the withdrawal of Swiss federal support for farmers.

I saw in Walter's situation a Swiss version of what I've seen repeatedly in Wisconsin. As farming has become increasingly market-oriented, increasingly a business and less and less a true homestead or cultural way of life, young people drift away. Well, if the purpose of farming is to make a living in a way that's essentially no different than working in a factory or office, then why farm? Why be tied to animals and land seven days a week when forty hours will do?

This is a perfectly legitimate question—except for that troublesome little "if."

"If" agriculture is only another industry, then we'll have to stop saying agri*culture* and say only agri*business*. But before we casually drop the culture out of agriculture, we might want to examine and consider just what it is we're letting go of.

Certainly some of what we're abandoning is a rural way of life of adequate population density and consistent practice that is (or was) complex enough to be a "culture." This is (or was) an *old* culture, changing and adjusting and adapting over the long haul, but old beyond memory, dating back to the Neolithic. It was the Industrial Revolution that essentially destroyed this culture—not in a day or a week or a year or even in a decade, but over the course of a couple centuries.

The question is: what price are we paying for the destruction of this culture? Well, massively enlarged urban areas, a countryside that's devoid of its own social cohesion, increasing reliance on huge vertically-integrated industries that are energy-intensive and oil-dependent, a wild increase in crime and a great rise in the vicarious adrenaline of spectator sports at all levels—to name a few of the negatives.

What would it take to restore rural culture? First it would take an acknowledgment that something has disappeared that should be restored. Then it would take some hard thinking and some decisive acting to reconstruct rural life in creative ways. In my view, the immediate need is to create a practice of cooperation and community on the farm itself.

In order to explain what I meant, I had to tell Walter about the farm I grew up on. So while we washed dishes, we talked.

Most of the farms in my neighborhood were made, starting with no fields and no buildings, by people of my parents' generation. My father and then, after they were married, my father and mother, built the farm on which my two brothers and I were raised.

My father started with a homemade log house, a log barn, and forty acres of land: brush, stumps, rocks, and swamp. He had no electricity, no tractor, and no money. He did have a strong body, a determined will, a horse or two, a hand plow, an axe, a grubhoe, a stoneboat, and occasionally some dynamite. This was in 1930. By 1940, he and my mother had half a dozen cows, a flock of chickens, a large garden, and a few cleared acres. By 1955, there were three boys, a new lumber barn, a frame house, a garage, a chicken house, a pigpen, a cement silo, a tractor, electricity, and close to forty acres cleared. By the late 1970s it was obvious that none of the sons was willing to carry on the farm as an economic enterprise. The farm was sold. Ten years later it was sold again. To ask why this particular farm went out of the family is really no different than to ask why a similar thing happened to thousands of other family farms.

We started with farms whose base was self-provisioning: the garden, dairy products, eggs, meat, firewood, maple syrup, wool, etc. These were farms, without electricity or internal combustion engines, in which the entire family worked at various tasks of subsistence. Surplus farm products were sold for necessary cash with which to buy those items which could not be produced on the farm.

There were various critical points in the economics—and *home* economics—of farming. Certainly the building of railroads was one, enabling the long-distance, cheap transport of food. The changes in technology during and after World War II made for another turning point: virtually all farms obtained electricity; virtually all farms obtained internal combustion engines—tractors, in particular—and an entire set of new machinery to match. Production was quickly expanded and the consumption of purchased commodities increased.

Within one generation—namely my own—the homestead base of family farming practically disappeared. Farming became increasingly a business. And since we kids were told over and over again that *farming is a business*—by magazines, by 4-H clubs, by the F.F.A. (Future Farmers of America), by farm organizations of all political stripes, by county agricultural agents, by teachers, by politicians, by county fairs, and by the behavior of our parents—we therefore concluded the obvious: namely, there were far easier ways to "make a living."

What practically everybody failed to notice was that the homestead, the self-provisioning aspect of farming, was the historical taproot of rural culture. With this taproot neglected, damaged and decayed, there was no coherent reason for young people to stay. All this happened mostly below the level of consciousness. We didn't think about it. But it was a felt thing. Emotionally, there was nothing to hold young people on the farms. Farming meant business. Business meant money. The culture was being stripped away from agriculture, and with it went the emotional ties. "Scientific" farming had only a condescending acquaintance with culture and no time for anything as drippy as "emotional ties." This was logical thinking and it didn't take a rocket scientist to figure it out.

In other words, our parents' generation, by buying into the marketplace and the Standard of Living at the expense of homestead culture, set the stage for us kids to abandon farming altogether. *They* may have thought they were building a real business to pass along. In fact, they did just the opposite: they abandoned the subsistence side (thus making us increasingly unfamiliar with its practices) and they vastly increased the business side (which, in our trained, indoctrinated and calculating eyes, was not viable).

There was a brief, critical moment, in my own later consideration of the farm, when I had an important discussion with my father. He was telling me that the farm was hardly big enough to support one family, and I was telling him that the farm needed more people, several families, to bring it back to life. He told me my idea was not practical. I told him that to make the farm a place of beauty, to explore its productive potential, to diversify but not to exceed the carrying capacity of the land, was a long-term task requiring a *community* base, with income coming into the farm from outside employment and professions but with a base of people left on the farm to work it as it should or could be worked. This would maximize self-provisioning, enable the exploration of cottage industry and alternative energy, allow for the time to make the place and the buildings as lovely as possible—a democratic manor, you might say, minus the manor lord.

And this points straightaway to its weakest spot: community-based homestead farming depends on wholesome cooperation and disciplined sharing. It depends on a level of open communication that is called for in the Christian gospels, that is hearkened to in the most passionate of democratic aspirations, but which is extremely difficult to achieve or sustain. Why? Because we are selfish human beings, because we are self-centered and tight-lipped and pushy and sneaky and greedy and unsatisfied and lustful. In other words, we are incapacitated by our limitations, by our sinfulness, from achieving a community-based cultural coherence. Simultaneously, we are bombarded by organized or institutional sin which pounds competitiveness into our heads, which literally seduces us through its extremely subtle advertising, which frowns on and eagerly crushes any stumbling attempt in the direction of subsistence community.

As the old community-of-necessity fell apart, we were "set free" randomly in the world to sink or swim or flounder or wallow or do whatever we chose or were drawn into. Meanwhile the "advances" in technology drove wedges more and more deeply between us and our past.

In a way, the Protestant Reformation set us up for this destruction of culture by technology in the hands of organized sin. The Protestants did away with monasteries and monastic life. That is to say, they deliberately did away with the lifelong practice of contemplation. This meant that our only models for living were to be found, in actual practice, in the world of economics—including the clergymen who were, after all, professionals like lawyers and doctors. The contemplative life, with its complementary side of community and cooperation and service, was suddenly no longer available even as a reminder of an alternative way of life, and perhaps a superior way of life.

So now we live in the muck of get and spend, and "Progress" is the name of our economic heaven. We have violence and crime and credit and drugs and political bankruptcy and extraordinary athletes and cheap food, cheap clothes, cheap oil, and the most superbly manufactured remote control VCR your plastic card can buy....

So, though he and his mother still own the farm, Walter does his farming through an intermediary. Meanwhile—single and never married—he is "shift leader" in a factory that recycles plastic containers, works lots of overtime, and takes extensive vacations to countries with old cultures: India, Nepal, Sri Lanka, Burma, Cambodia, Laos, China, and once to Cuba. Next on the itinerary is Mongolia.

Eventually it became clear that Walter is drawn toward Buddhism—partly his travels, partly the influence of Elsbeth's and Vater's sister Lena, who lives in an ashram right smack in Winterthur. (At this point in the conversation, Walter went to fetch a book to show me: *The Autobiography of a Yogi* by Paramahansa Yogananda, published originally in English in—wouldn't you know?—the United States, in 1946.) He tends to believe that life is too complicated to be contained by a single incarnation. Therefore there are former lives and future lives; but to know about them, or to try to know about them, is irrelevant and a waste of time. "Za only zing ve can do eez vork on ourselves. Zat eez our zhab. Zees I believe."

Tante Elsbeth gave to Susanna a traditional Swiss dress that she was otherwise going to give to a thrift store: Tante Elsbeth quit wearing traditional clothes when she got married; her husband told her it made her look like a farmer, and that was an embarrassment.

By nine o'clock it was evident that Tante Elsbeth was growing tired—golly gee whiz! *I* was tired, what with all this concentrated conversation!—and so Walter rearranged the junk in his tiny Renault (it was wonderful to discover an untidy Swiss) and drove us to

Götighofen. Which is a little, maybe, like what karma is: "Vork on ourselves. Zat eez our zhab. Zees I believe." Rearrange the junk. Recycle your way of life. Subsist on the past. Waltz with balding bears named Valter.

Tuesday mid-morning
February 13

Outside this third-floor bedroom window, big flakes of snow are swirling and swooping and being tossed about by a wind that blows in fits and starts. Yet, somehow, when it really matters, the weather is exactly right—like yesterday.

We could already see the Säntis, and a whole long range of lesser, adjoining mountains, before we left, shortly after nine o'clock, to get Mama from the *Altersheim*. It wasn't sunny, and it never became sunny all day, but the air was remarkably *klar*, clear.

Mama had an appointment in the hospital in Münsterlingen, with the doctor who replaced her worn-out hip last fall. From Sulgen we went north through Leimbach to Mattwil. From Mattwil to Langrickenbach we drove on the crown of a hill, headed northeast, and a whole range of Alps was clearly visible all the way into Austria: but from this perspective, the mountains were scenic and even cute, picturesque, not cold and awesome and merciless as they were from the frigid summit of the Säntis.

From Langrickenbach north through Zuben, Schönenbaumgarten ("beautiful tree garden"), to Scherzingen, the Bodensee—or Lake Constance, as it's also called—was clearly visible, with Germany dark and shaggy on the far shore.

Münsterlingen is a small town right on the lake. Vater drove right up to the *Spital*, the hospital; Susanna and I walked Mama in, while Vater parked the car. We waited till Vater came in, walked them both to their waiting room, said goodbye, and left.

Our first stop was an old Catholic church next door. The door was unlocked, but the main body of the church, the nave, was blocked by a sliding metal grate, closed and locked. On a pedestal, just behind the grate, was a painted head (of wood? of plaster?) of St. John the Evangelist, with an expression of sweet, ironic amusement. An inscription explained that when next the Bodensee freezes over (the last time was in 1963), this head of St. John will be carried in great procession across the ice to a sister church in Germany, and left there, until the Bodensee freezes once again, and St. John will return here, to Switzerland. Perhaps John's expression reflects his mute embarrassment with all the excessive disembodied fanfare.

The head of St. John The Evangelist.

We then crossed the street and walked alongside a long complex of modern but tasteful buildings which border the lake, buildings which house an apparently rather large population of psychiatric patients, a psychiatric clinic, and a school for psychiatric nurses. A young fellow at a sewing machine, sewing on a rag rug, fairly glared at us out a window. Toward the end of this complex we were waved to another exit under the nurses' school by a young man in blaze orange who was directing foot traffic away from several huge trees where a half-dozen other young men in blaze orange vests were pruning

Psychiatric masonry in Münsterlingen.

branches with hand tools, high up in the trees. I paused there to take a photograph of a wonderfully loony sculpture, made of rocks and cement, that I quickly dubbed "psychiatric masonry." (As a stone mason myself, I now know where to come when I go over the edge.)

At the lake shore I found a fine fist-sized rock to take back to Wisconsin: it will go into the stone wall of the porch we intend to build onto the log house.

It was only a short walk to the *Bahnhof*. Susanna bought us our (half-price) tickets to St. Gallen. In a few minutes the *Zug* arrived, we got on, and left.

The train to Romanshorn hugs the lake shore. The distance between the tracks and the shore was never great, but what was in that space varied considerably. There were small fields and vineyards, orchards and pastures with grazing sheep. There were farms and old houses. There were new houses, a marina, villages, and three or four very tidy trailer parks, ugly as plucked ducks. These were the first trailers I've seen in Switzerland.

The train went on to Rorschach, at the south end of the Bodensee, not far from where the Rhine flows in. But we got off at Romanshorn.

Romanshorn! This name keeps bothering and agitating me. Roman's Horn! There must be some fantastic history of ancient Rome associated with the place, for surely the Roman legions came down the Rhine to the Bodensee. Those whom I've so far asked—including Vater—only shrug and say, "You'll have to ask an historian," though at breakfast this morning Vater did say that, in Zürich, there is a museum with replicas of lake houses on stilts built by some prehistoric people. Roman's Horn!

The *Bahnhof* at Romanshorn lies right up against the tiny harbor. In the harbor, taking on its cargo of passengers and vehicles, was moored the German ferry *Friedrichshafen*, a white boat two hundred feet long and fifty feet wide, and we ran to catch it, the very last passengers, barely in the nick of time.

We were hardly on board before we could feel the quiet, powerful surge of engines. We stood (and never went into the warm restaurant on the way over or on the way back) on the upper deck, right below the pilot's cabin, the ducks and gulls distancing

The Friedrichshafen *at dock in Romanshorn.*

themselves from the boat as the pilot smoothly ran us out of the green harbor water, through an opening in the breakwater, and out into the black *Wasser* of the Bodensee.

We had run on board without tickets. Soon, a tall, thin man in blue pants and coat, in a white cap with blue visor, strode up to us. He had a thin, short, grey-blonde beard. He was German. He was fussy and officious. He complained that our half-price documents were almost run out. (They were good until February 24....) He was, in short, a self-important jerk, the sort of character who gives German movies a bad name.

We were standing on the port or larboard side. We moved to starboard so we could see the *wunderbar* mountains to the south and southeast. There we literally bumped into a middle-aged German fellow with greying muttonchops who told Susanna there wasn't much to see in Friedrichshafen (the town in Germany to which we were headed) because the Americans had bombed it ninety-five percent *kaputt*, that the lake was deep and somewhere in its depths was an airplane. I asked Susanna to ask what it was that made

The author on deck.

Friedrichshafen a target for bombing, but the man moved away—but whether because he was cold (he had been holding his coat collar up to his face to protect it from the breeze), or because he didn't like the American in the red wool coat, wasn't ever clear.

These two encounters, unanticipated and tight together, worked like a magnet to polarize an entire field of old, old feelings which were shaped in my childhood. Five of my uncles were in the U.S. military in World War II, and I literally grew up in the emotional fumes of evil Germany crushed at last in its unrepentant wickedness.

I stood at the rail the entire time the ferry surged across the Bodensee toward Germany—eleven or twelve kilometers in forty minutes—and these old feelings rolled and tumbled inside me. I felt my jaw tighten. My mother's people all came from Germany—my mother never spoke English until she was seven years old and had to go to school—and I was, in a sense, on my maiden voyage to my Motherland, and what I felt was a wary, tense hostility. *Wahnsinnig!*

Tuesday night

A writer, for no better reason than that his pen gets bumped, can change subjects, just like that. Actually, my reason is partly accident and partly design. The accident is that Walter Hut ("Valter Hoot") came at precisely 12:30 to take Susanna and me to Winterthur, to visit

Tante Lena in her ashram—the Omkarananda Ashram, no less. The design, or maybe just fickle impulse, is to leave both the writer and the reader freezing their butts off on the upper deck of the German ferry *Friedrichshafen*, churning across the black Bodensee toward *Deutschland*, with an analogous churning going on within—and to turn about and write between times a brief account of an encounter with "DLZ", Divine Light Mission, and Universal Love. (Actually, "DLZ" stands for Divine Light *Zentrum*—Divine Light Center—but Divine Light Mission will also do.)

It was maybe two o'clock when we arrived—a Swiss, a half-Swiss, and a true blue American (an "Ami," in Swiss slang), in a tiny purple French car with Appenzeller yodeling on the tape deck, on a visit to a sweet seventy year-old Swiss Tante in a Hindu ashram headed by a Swami from India whom Swiss authorities consider a criminal because of certain, ahem, financial indiscretions.

Far out. I guess that's the only thing to say. Far out!

Tante Lena, it seems fair to say, has found her niche (from the Latin *nidus*, meaning nest) in the OM of the universe.

Who am I?
Before I was born, I was.
After I die, I will be.
A timeless Being
came from, and into,
timeless Eternity.
Time was formed,
and time is dissolved,
and I remain
what I have always been,
a Being with depths to which
there is no beginning,
and heights
to which there is no end.

–Swami Omkarananda

That little poem (if that's what it is) may not have quite the zip of this one—

Grandpa's whiskers old and grey
often get in Gramma's way.
Once she chewed them in her sleep,
thinking they were shredded wheat.

–Burma Shave

—but for all the sticky, spongy, excessive "profundity," there may well be in the DLZ a serious determination to incorporate the Divine into every aspect of life, to live a life of compassion and caring and service. And that deserves our respect, even with all the syrup—and maybe even with the corruption.

Tante Lena, warm and welcoming, met us at the back door of the ashram. She ushered us all into a small dining room in which the

Tante Lena in the ashram.

colors blue, pink, and white predominated. The floor was dark blue linoleum tile. The tabletops were dark blue. The curtains were dark blue. The walls and ceiling were white. Pink, shades and patterns of pink, was the color of the cloths that draped the huge, framed, color photograph of the Swami (dark hair, glasses, white robe, left profile) and the huge, framed picture of two Hindu gods.

Walter left, but not because he's not close to Tante Lena. Walter left, that's all I know, and he didn't come back for two hours. Meanwhile, Tante Lena served us coffee and cookies at one of the white tables with a blue top. We sat on white chairs, and for quite a while I read in the little devotional booklet from which I copied the Swami's poem from the back cover. Susanna and Tante Lena talked about family things in *Schweizerdeutsch*.

Tante Lena is rather small, with thin brown-grey hair. She was dressed in—what else?—pink and blue. (Oddly enough, and certainly not by design, Susanna was dressed in pink and blue, and I was dressed in maroon and blue. Walter, the plump Buddhist, wore blue jeans and a black leather jacket. There were little yellow boxes of cigars on the dash of his purple Renault.)

There's not a lot to report. Tante Lena—her ashram name is Pranava—is a mild, elderly woman who's found her place, who meditates and has her mantras, who strives to fill her entire being with the Divine. Actually, that's a whole lot to report. I respect her odd, brave choice.

Out of two small speakers came an unending loop of chanting. This was always in the background—not exactly soothing—hypnotic would be more accurate. But this is intentional, for the function of the mantra is to "dissolve the mind" of distractions and wicked thoughts: "Beat it from all sides with the Mantra, so that if you open your eyes or close your eyes you will see only the Light, only the Divine."

The chanting stirred a memory, and I finally figured out what it was: an old field recording, done in the deep South, of black men setting railroad tracks by hand. One man was the chanter who set the rhythm of the work—lifting in unison, hammering in alternating strokes—and the remaining workers were the chorus, moving with the rhythm, keeping time, *forgetting* time in the awful heat of heavy labor and sunstroke. And it was this latter function, the need to avoid clock time and not become desperate and frantic in the brutal hardness of labor and heat, that tied it in my mind to the hypnotic Hindu chanting: which made me wonder why, given the background of black men in America, there are Black Muslims but not Black Hindus...? But then in India there is caste (the word derives from the Portuguese *casta*, meaning race or lineage) and black folks have been squeezed out the bottom of the caste system into untouchability, which is a glass ceiling with a vengeance.

Walter returned, we said our warm goodbyes to Tante Lena. She gave Susanna and me each a little square of blessed chocolate, once held in the Swami's very own hands. I slipped mine into my coat pocket (Susanna slipped hers into her mouth) and then we folded ourselves into the little purple car with the yellow boxes of cigars on the dash. Cheerfully talking about Swiss politics and Swiss farming practices (the Swiss President is a powerless figurehead; many dairy farmers don't use silos because a lot of cheese is made from raw milk and silage ruins the taste) Walter drove us rapidly to Sulgen, dropping us off at Mama's *Altersheim*. Walter left, with our fond goodbyes. Susanna and I visited Mama. Vater came, we talked, we left, and that's the day.

May your nighttime OM be mellow. *Schlaf wohl.* I'll see you tomorrow morning on the cold metal deck of the *Friedrichshafen*.

Wednesday morning
February 14

Guten Morgen, Damen und Herren! On your left, to the northwest, please observe the dark, slightly breeze-rumpled *Wasser* of the Bodensee, with here and there a solitary fisherman in a small boat, a slowly-flapping large grey-white gull, and a gliding *Kormoran*. On your right, off the starboard rail, please note the scenic snow-covered mountains that begin shortly beyond the bottom (or is it the top?) of the Bodensee and that sprawl off into *Österreich*, Austria. And

The harbor in Friedrichshafen, Germany.

straight ahead, closer with every throb of the engine, with every spin of the propeller, comes the beloved *Mutterland von dem Vaterland....*

No. For me, Germany is my mother's land. Austria is my father's land. *Österreich ist mein Vaterland.* The personalities of my parents—my mother restless, impatient, ambitious; my father stolid, hard-working, largely content with a peasant's life and comforts—are all mixed up in my internal churning. We jumped onto this ferry on a lark, on an impulse, and everything within me is rising against this dark land whose harbor, whose large masonry breakwater, we now approach.

The pilot slows the engine and we glide through the watergate into calm green water. A few hundred yards more and the pilot smoothly rolls the ferry to port, and we come with hardly a bump to the dock. A ramp is lowered by electric motor; engines are started in the vehicles on board. We disembark up the ramp.

At the head of the ramp stand two customs police in uniforms of distinctive green who carefully check our passports and inquire unsmilingly how long we are staying.

Old cafe in Friedrichshafen.

We were both rather chilled, so we began at once to look for a cafe where we might have a cup of coffee. From the ferry, while still out in the lake, we had thought a section of buildings along the waterfront looked old. We walked there, the lake on our left; but we soon discovered that what had looked traditional and old from a distance was really quite new—with two small, genuinely old buildings tucked between. These were charming if also a touch shabby. There were cafes, but too modern for our taste. We kept walking into the adjoining streets—cobblestone, rather narrow, curving, no motorized traffic, a little dirty, with buildings three and four stories tight together, "old" in superficial style but all in various pastel shades, stucco, busy with shoppers in the multitude of shops.

Eventually we found our way into a basement cafe called *Spitalkeller*, "hospital cellar," which had an arched ceiling of uneven white plaster and walls of white plaster with random stones showing through. It was a fairly small room, with benches and booths, tables and chairs, around the perimeter in a pleasing pattern. We sat in a booth. The waitress came, was very friendly, and Susanna ordered for me (for herself she wanted only coffee) a plate of *Krautschupfnudeln* and a cup of coffee.

The food came in reasonable time, on a large warm white plate. It consisted of a large heap of small, dense noodles, boiled and then fried with bits of bacon, tossed with hot sauerkraut, and garnished with parsley. And rather salty. That's it. Frankly, it needed a serving of cold pickled beets, a fat slice of hot caraway rye bread with melted butter, and a frosty mug of good dark beer—but none of this did I have.

It was good. I ate, we talked, Susanna asked for the bill. The waitress came and Susanna paid with Swiss money, a Fr.50.00 note. The waitress said "Excuse me," and left. When she came back (and, to her credit, I thought she was embarrassed) she said her boss had said fine, one for one, with change in German marks.

I regret to this very moment that I let it slide. One for one was by no stretch of the imagination a fair exchange, for Swiss currency is, as they say in money speak, much "stronger." So this anonymous boss—whoever he was—not only burned us on the paying end, he also added insult to injury by returning change in German currency. So if you're ever in Friedrichshafen, and you go into a little basement restaurant called *Spitalkeller*, and if you don't happen to have German marks on you, go *first* to the big boss and get the price straight—and, if you don't like the arrangement, tell him so and leave. Tell him an *amerikanisch Nebelhorn* sent you. And tell him, too, to serve cold pickled beets and hot caraway rye bread drenched in butter with the *Krautschupfnudeln*. And don't forget the dark beer.

We had nearly an hour before the ferry was to leave. So we walked to the big church with the twin cupolas farther up the shoreline. A large area of this intervening space was city park and walkway. There were gulls and ducks and a few big white swans with black faces in the water, at the shoreline: they would gather in a rush, gulls swooping, when anyone offered food.

We never got inside the church grounds. A huge parklike yard with lawn and massive beech trees was inside a very high old stone wall, with here and there tall metal gates to peer through. The church itself was huge, of grey stone. We hurried back, Susanna bought a couple pieces of bakery—*Plunder*, sort of a cinnamon roll, and a slice of *Oma's Käsekuchen*, literally "Gramma's cheesecake"—and we got aboard the ferry. I tossed a tidbit overboard to a swan and instantly the gulls came swooping and two or three kinds of ducks began paddling toward us. Several times the gulls snatched in mid-air the tidbits Susanna and I threw down to the swan.

The ferry got underway, we glided through the watergate, our tickets were checked by a very friendly, ruddy-faced Swiss—also in dark blue with a white cap and blue visor—and we went quickly (the

Bodensee was slightly rougher) back to Romanshorn.

As we slid into the harbor, I told Susanna I was glad to be back in Switzerland. "Ey-yi-yi," said Susanna, "five weeks in Switzerland and already you get homesick when you leave for one little afternoon!" We both laughed; but I think she, too, was glad to be back.

Naturally the train to St. Gallen left *right now*. So we once again made a dash for it and, like so often on this trip, made it barely in the nick of time.

Twenty minutes and two tunnels later we got off at the *Bahnhof* in St. Gallen. We bought tickets—St. Gallen to Sulgen—did a little quick shopping (found a few Segantini cards, for one thing) and partially retraced our way through the old city and up the other side—literally up the other very steep side—to meet the people who had invited us to supper, Herr Walter Sutter and Frau Helen Sutter, singers in the Bach choir Vater organized and directed for over forty years. Naturally they had to live on the sixth floor....

The Sutters are fairly short and slim people in their mid-sixties. Both are lively and very attentive. She is rather wrinkled, her hair grey-black. He looks far younger than he is, with an almost irrepressible leprechaun energy under a shaggy mop of thick white hair.

Why did they invite us? Well, they know Susanna somewhat through Vater and Mama; so partly it was to find out, discreetly, how Mama and Vater are doing. Partly they are simply curious, interested—wanting to know about America, about our lives in Wisconsin, and (especially from me as a newcomer) impressions of Switzerland. We had a tour of the apartment (seventy percent of Swiss people rent, said Herr Sutter) and wine and conversation, some of it huddled around a map of Wisconsin. Everyone is terribly impressed that we live in the woods with deer, bear, bobcat, and wolves.

And then the fondue was ready, and the bread, and more wine, and more fondue, the conversation mostly in English but lapsing frequently into Swiss-German, and then a fruit salad with nuts, and, for me, some orange-flavored cognac in a glass that must be held in the hands to warm, just so. *Wunderbar.* But, since I drink alcohol so infrequently, a little does a big job inside my sober *amerikanisch* body, and I had to be careful lest my *Nebelhorn* toot too much too loud.

But we had yet another train to catch. Hurriedly we said goodbye and thank you to Frau Sutter, fairly ran down the stairs with Herr Sutter, walked quickly through the new slushy snow to the garage where the Sutters' car was parked, and he drove us to the *Bahnhof* in great cheerfulness, our seat belts carefully fastened. We said goodbye, shook hands goodbye, waved goodbye, and we were actually early (by maybe two minutes) in the second-class coach.

This was a *Schnellzug*, a fast train, to Winterthur. We had to get off and change trains (we thought) at Gossau. On the platform at Gossau, Susanna quickly read the schedule—no train! But there was reference to a bus and we hurried once again, running down steps and under the tracks and back up more steps on the far side; and there in the parking lot was our bus, door open, ready to go. We ran to it, splashing through the slush. Puffing, Susanna began to dig in her purse for the tickets, but the bus driver, with cheerful nonchalance, waved us in, laughing, saying he didn't need to see our tickets, not to worry. He was a jolly man with a big mustache; and when we got out at Sulgen—it was by then almost ten o'clock—I thanked him with my poor, stumbling *Schweizerdeutsch*, and he called back some cheerful parting words and waved to us as he pulled away.

What a purely wonderful thing cheerfulness is! How it lightens and brightens the heart!

With lightness and brightness in our hearts, Susanna and I walked in murky darkness to Götighofen. The sand truck was out, its yellow lights flashing. I hoped to hear an owl, but didn't.

Vater in his striped nightshirt was waiting up for us, let us in, and was both astonished and delighted by the adventures of our day.

But the next morning, at breakfast, he repeated and underscored what Herr Sutter had told us in St. Gallen: Friedrichshafen, home of the blimpmeister Count Ferdinand von Zeppelin, produced military aircraft, and *that's* why it was bombed by the Americans—the Americans, who, under anti-aircraft fire, managed to spare two big churches. Vater said the air raids took place at night, late in the war; you could hear the American planes in the night sky (he made a long, uncanny rumble that started deep in his big chest), and the entire Bodensee was illuminated by fire and flare and bomb blast.

What quirk of fate brought me ashore at Friedrichshafen, at this *kaputt* military center, my mother's *Vaterland*? Why am I so intrigued by the name "Romanshorn"?

On the ferry, on our way back to Switzerland, Susanna explained to me that the cheesecake was *"Oma's,"* Gramma's; that *"Oma"* and *"Opa"* are typical German endearing nicknames for Gramma (*"Omama"*) and Grampa (*"Opapa"*); that these terms can be made more endearing yet by saying *"Omali"* and *"Opali"*—Little Gramma and Little Grampa.

So Susanna, who is already twice a "Little Gramma," has become to me, with an added optional layer of ashram OM, an *Omali*. So to these puzzling quirks of fate, this unanswerable fascination, I can only say I was brought here by my own little *Omali, Mutterland* of my heart. Ommm - ommmm - ommmmmali....

Friday morning
February 16

Some days are as sweet and mild as a baby's sleep, during which the entire universe seems to gently rock. Wednesday was such a day. Life was for Being, not for Act. I wrote. Susanna sent postcards. Vater had a voice student from St. Gallen. We all visited Mama at the *Altersheim*. Everything was slow and easy.

On the *Bahnhof* platform at Sulgen, Thursday morning, Susanna and I had just finished singing Bill Staines' song "River" to an audience of empty engines, when a *Schnellzug* to Romanshorn roared past, throwing up and leaving in its wake a veritable blizzard of fine snow. Though I didn't realize it at the time, this was an omen for the day.

At 8:14 exactly, we were on the train to St. Gallen. Shortly after nine—we had a little trouble finding Annemarie and her little red car—we were on our way out of St. Gallen bound for the Rhine valley, past Rorschach to St. Margrethen.

Snow was falling when Vater drove us from Götighofen to

Sulgen. It was heavily overcast all the way to St. Gallen. But coming down into the Rhine valley there was faint gauzy sunshine with—well, one can hardly say "ground fog" because the ground was snow-covered—snow fog, *Schneenebel*. Part of this highway was *Autobahn*, meaning dual-lane, divided with a median, limited access, and fast. The fog, the glare, the speed, the conversation, and the relative flatness of the landscape combined to make this portion of the trip less than scenic.

But then I saw the Rhine—narrower and smaller than I'd somehow imagined (perhaps the size of the Wisconsin River as it flows through Rhinelander), but totally canalized and diked ("made to behave," was how Susanna put it), jade-green in color, very much like the Aare. The highway followed rather tightly the west bank of the Rhine. Across the Rhine was *Österreich, mein Vaterland*.

At one point the highway was being rebuilt. Several men were constructing a stone wall with black rocks as big as refrigerators. These rocks were hoisted into place by a backhoe on cat tracks. Two or three men on the wall were guiding the stones with poles and levers. The finished wall was maybe ten feet high, four or five feet across at the top, and much wider at the base. No cement was used—the rocks were rough but fitted—and Susanna pointed out a similar wall a moment later that was overgrown with ivy. The wall was obviously there to enclose and muffle the road.

By the time we had come opposite Liechtenstein, by Buchs, the fog was above us and the sky was, for the time being, cloudy, and the light less glary.

"Here we go into Liechtenstein," said Annemarie, as she took an exit from the highway.

"Will we need to show passports?" I asked, reaching for my wallet.

"Ny-ny," Annemarie replied. "Liechtenstein is on very friendly terms with the Swiss people." After which remark Susanna and Annemarie discussed (we went up and over the Rhine) the use in Liechtenstein of the Swiss franc. There was not even a hint of a checkpoint.

We were quickly in Schann. I somehow expected something

(Above) The Lord of Liechtenstein's
wine cellar.

(Left) The Lord of Liechtenstein's
castle overlooking the city of Vaduz.

older, and I was frankly disappointed by the relatively unimaginative modern houses. The cars had black license plates with the letters
FL (*Fürstentum Liechtenstein,* "Lorddom of Light Stone") and numbers in white. We drove south to Vaduz, parking briefly in the
Lordship's vineyard (it said so on a big sign), and I took a photograph of the castle perched high above the town. While Annemarie,
with her throaty laugh, went looking for "a royal garbage can" in
which to toss the paper towel she'd used to wipe the windshield,
Susanna stood gazing up at the castle. Finally she said, "Ah, I can see
His Highness in the dining room. He's eating breakfast but he's mad
because the salt's not on the table for his eggs."

"Ya, ya, ya," we all said, laughing, as we got back into the
Japanese car parked in His Lordship's vineyard.

Liechtenstein is a Catholic country. Annemarie pointed out the
big church as we drove out of Vaduz—pronounced "fa-doots." By
the time we were past Triesen, on our way to Balzers, the sky had

begun to clear. At Balzers, just before we crossed again into Switzerland, Annemarie pointed out another castle, this one set on the crown of a steep little hill between Balzers and the Rhine, owned by a famous movie actress; but Annemarie, whose familiarity with popular culture is not exactly great, couldn't remember who.

We crossed the unattended border and began at once to climb, headed slightly southeast, through a lovely area controlled by the Swiss military. The first sign of this control was a thick, irregular wall of concrete: a wall to prevent the passage of tanks, Annemarie explained, built during World War II.

Mountains rose to our left (east) and right (west). We passed an army training area on our right—there was a squad of men in a snowy yard and another man, in a snowy meadow, putting a magnificent riding horse through its paces—and Annemarie said that *in* the mountain beyond the training area were military caverns and depots, "very secret." We passed another tank wall, fronted by a pit, went through a very narrow archway, past a small woods of huge twisted old, old oaks, steadily down now toward Maienfeld—Heidi country.

I was stunned. We had passed into another climate, another culture, another century. We were in an old *italienisch* town with stone walls and stone fences and old buildings and tortuously twisting, narrow cobblestone streets, and miles of grapevines carefully, meticulously trellised. Annemarie zipped up and around these wonderful wicked streets with utterly blind corners and unexpected fountains until my knuckles were white from a strange blend of fear and esthetic paralysis. *Wahnsinnigwunderbar!*

We drove next to Malans, which was something of a repeat performance of Maienfeld: old, *italienisch* in feeling, narrow, twisting and turning, stone fences, rock walls. After one dead end, Annemarie took us into the courtyard, or backyard, of an old, somewhat decrepit, huge, sprawling manor house, home to an old schoolmate of Annemarie's, Flandrina von Salis—Salis from *Salix*, which is Latin for willow.

These two towns, this little region, Annemarie explained, still carries the name *"Herrschaftsland,"* which has overtones of an old aristocracy, of manor lords.

From Malans we dropped quickly southwest a few kilometers to Landquart (the town), turned left to follow upstream the Landquart River, and passed through a tunnel to the long, narrow valley known as the Prättigau. The tunnel is relatively new (how new I don't know), but it was obviously made with modern machinery, given its length and finish. The point is, the old entrance to the Prättigau was in a *Klus*, a very steep and narrow gorge through which the Landquart tumbles—and, undoubtedly in the spring, roars. This is a valley with a natural gate, in other words.

So here again we entered a region with its own history, its own microclimate, its own way of doing things. The people were mostly poor farmers, Annemarie said, many of them claiming descent from the semi-mythical Walsers.

In fact, first stop for us past Schiers and Jenaz was Küblis, home village to the Juons, where the family is registered, including Susanna and all her children, though not one of them has ever lived there for who knows how many generations. The older houses in the Prättigau were of heavily weathered wood, some of round logs, some of hewn logs, and completely unlike the *italienisch* houses in *Herrschaftsland*.

From Küblis, Annemarie took us up an extremely narrow asphalt road, with many hairpin turns, and edges you most certainly would not want to drop a wheel over—all this back in the general direction of Schiers—until high above the valley we entered the tiny village of Putz (pronounced "pootz") where there was a little restaurant recommended to Annemarie by Herr Walter Sutter, the St. Gallen leprechaun with white hair. This restaurant was so inconspicuous that we had to find a slightly wider place in the road to turn around and return to Putz to hunt for it.

But then we did find it—we'd driven right past it before—an old, old set of farm buildings, house and barn built tight together in the familiar manner, with a hefty, steaming manure pile out front, a flock of colorful, free-ranging chickens, and no obvious door to enter. Across the road, perched right on the edge of the more or less flat land, before the mountainside fell away down, down, down, was the

Castels in Putz.

overgrown remains of a fort or castle built of grey stone. The name of the restaurant, on the farmhouse wall above where the chickens were scratching, was "Castels."

A little footpath was discovered which went round the side of the farmhouse, and up through some bushes. There we found an open, wooden porch, and a broad, short, old wooden door with an ancient latch. Annemarie tried the door. It was locked. She knocked. A tall, lean, broad-shouldered man opened the door and inquired, without great warmth or interest, what it was we wanted. He had very short dark hair, was clean-shaven, and his face was a sober mask of extremely strong features. He was, perhaps, thirty years old, wearing a white shirt and black pants, with a white apron that fell almost to his ankles. He had very strong hands and extremely long fingers.

We were ushered in (I had to duck my head), stumbled down two old steps, and walked into a dim hallway with very large, reasonably flat, black flagstones for a floor. On the right was a short, arched doorway into the kitchen. The odors that poured out were wonderful. On the left, up another step or two, was an old wooden door, also wide and short, through which we were taken to a dining room perhaps two hundred and fifty years old. The only ugly thing in the room was the chocolate-brown floor rug, rather badly in need of the attention of a dustsucker.

The room was otherwise almost entirely finished with wood—wood ornamented and carved, with another door low and wide, four beautifully inlaid tables with slate centers, lovely wooden chairs and cushioned benches, a dark, carved hutch in a corner with several bottles of liqueur, an assortment of candles, a cluster of newspapers, and a few antique plates. The low wooden ceiling was a maze of trim. There also was an old tile stove which had white plaster where the tiles should have been.

The overall effect was of charming, rustic elegance rather run-down at the heels, but aristocratic enough to be a little demanding about manners—not the genteel, snobbish manners that are repulsed by *Mist* (manure) that steams by the barn or by chickens that poop on the porch, but a deeper and older kind of courtesy that is both respectful and a little tough.

The chef—our lean, dark doorman in the white apron—brought to our table a vase of fresh flowers, the menu, and, grasping very quickly that one of his guests was an American, asked with a perfectly straight face that nevertheless betrayed a totally malicious intent whether I might "like a Coke?"

The formality was immediately lessened by our hearty laughter. But not giving up so easily, the chef then asked, upon learning my interest in wine, whether I would prefer one liter or two? One could not help but sense his low opinion of Americans.

Susanna and Annemarie decided on *Capuns* ("ka-poons") for us all. The chef brought tea, cold lemon-flavored water, a dry red wine, and homemade dark bread. We sat and chatted, looked at the three small windows made with round glass sections, thick like the bottoms of wine bottles. Curtains hung on handmade curtain rods. Within twenty minutes, perhaps, our formal, sardonic chef brought us each a very large plate of this Graubünden specialty: a homemade noodle dough, with sausage, steamed in a wrapping of Swiss chard, and modestly drenched with a cream sauce. We ate with relish and a will. The silverware was large and unusually heavy.

When next the chef came in to see how we were doing—we were the only diners—a shaggy calico cat with terribly matted fur came in with him, and stayed. The cat jumped up on a cushioned bench near Susanna, licked itself a few times, and promptly fell asleep.

We finished our meal, using the wonderful heavy dark bread to sop up the sauce. The dishes were removed. Dessert was next—different flavors of delicious ice cream, little chocolate cakes, and a custard—and consumed with loving appreciation, along with cups of delicious coffee.

The chef at Castels.

Annemarie went out to pay—she once again was treating Susanna and me to the day—so I woke the calico and fed her a little container of cream, about the volume of a large thimble. The cat instantly became my immediate and lifelong friend, snuggled up, and purred.

The handsome, tall, grave, sardonic chef walked us to the outer door and said goodbye. We strolled in the glorious sunshine, past chickens fluffing themselves in their sunny dust holes, to the little red car, got in and hairpinned our way down to Schiers—full, happy, and glowing.

Saturday morning
February 17

Shall I tell you from which walnut table I write, this glorious, grey, snow-falling day? No? OK, that will come later. In our fertile imaginations we therefore return to a speeding little red car, zipping down a valley highway alongside the tumbling Landquart River, headed west toward the Rhine, high snow-covered mountains rising to the north and south. Inside the car are the driver, an almost-retired Swiss doctor, and two passengers: a half-Swiss nurse with greying hair, perfectly fluent in two languages, and a balding, red-bearded Ami scribblemeister, increasingly inarticulate in one.

Back through the tunnel that parallels the *Klus*, past Landquart (the town) to the highway heading south, up the Rhine valley to Chur, pronounced "coor" with a little k-sound that scrapes in the throat. We drove through Chur, with its fine old buildings, and on its west side a concentrated area of pure ugliness consisting mainly of automobile dealerships with brazen signs and, the arch hamburger ambassador to the world, Ronald McDonald in blue and red plastic person.

At Chur, the Rhine valley proper turns in an amazingly straight line toward the southwest. This is the direction we went, until we turned south along the Hinterrhine by Bonaduz. Just before we arrived at the juncture of the Rhine and Hinterrhine, however, we swept round a long, lazy southwest-turning curve in the highway. Here, built atop a sturdy fence, were side-by-side solar panels that ran the entire length of the curve. (These were the only solar panels I've so far seen in Switzerland.)

We went south toward Thusis—a narrow valley—the green fast-flowing Hinterrhine—mountains rising on either side, with villages and small towns perched here and there, old castles, some of which were perilously sited on the crowns of terribly steep hills and rocky outcroppings. Annemarie pointed out the castle where Jürg Jenatsch, in 1621, took part in the murder of the Catholic leader Pompey Planta, during Switzerland's stormy participation in the Thirty Years'

War that wrecked much of Europe. (I happened to know some of this story because Susanna had given me the novel *Jürg Jenatsch*, by the Swiss writer Conrad Ferdinand Meyer, several years ago.)

Beginning at Thusis, Annemarie took us on the most incredible drive I, at least, have ever been on in my life. From Thusis to Zillis, the next town farther south, the Hinterrhine goes through an absolutely wicked gorge called a *Schlucht*. The tiny road that clings by its tire

The Viamala.

treads to the mountainside is named *Viamala*, which means "the bad way" and is totally deserving of the name. There were a couple tunnels hacked through rock, very roughly hewn, like goblin passageways in the scary adventures of Bilbo Baggins, Esquire. This was raw material for *Alptraum*, nightmares.

The gorge, the *Schlucht*, was a jagged V. Sometimes the Hinterrhine was visible among the boulders below, sometimes not. It was fabulous and scary. I recommend it as an absolute reprieve from boredom.

Once through this *phantastisch* playpen for trolls, we entered quite suddenly into yet another microclimate and mini-culture under the sheltering arms of macro-mountains. First stop, an old, old stone church in Zillis by the name of St. Martin. I most certainly would have guessed Catholic, but the rooster on the steeple crowed Protestant. Yet it was, or had been, a Catholic church in pre-Reformation Switzerland. The old, low, wide door (in old Switzerland there may be no other kind) was wooden and unadorned and considerably beat up. One had to step up to go over the sill—and duck to avoid a thump on the head—and then down two stone steps.

This was, bar none, the most beautiful, the most simple, wonderful, and worshipful church I have ever been in. It was small. In proportion it was long and narrow and fairly high. In the front where the altar would normally be (there was no altar but only a box of benches for confirmands or a choir and a baptismal font hewed roughly out of a huge stone) there was a gothic arched ceiling of whitewashed masonry with light grey trim. The walls everywhere were white plaster, the floor of cut grey stone wonderfully fitted. The pews were long

St. Martin's in Zillis, with Susanna and Annemarie.

wooden benches over a plank floor. There was a pipe organ, fairly new, rather small, mostly of wood. The carved wooden pulpit was fastened to the wall several feet above floor level. Over the pews, the organ, and the pulpit was a flat ceiling, maybe twenty feet up, completely covered with painted panels dating from the twelfth century. The panels were square, tight together in rows nine wide by seventeen long. Each panel was a biblical scene. Some were in sequence and told a story: the birth of Jesus, for instance, or Herod's murder of the boy children in and around Bethlehem. The building was unheated and cold, but we lingered, quietly, until shivering got the best of us.

We had one more town to go to—Andeer, a few kilometers farther south, also along the Hinterrhine. The sun was slipping behind a mountain, the top of which was a spumy roostertail of

The Town of Andeer.

wind-blown snow. There was essentially no snow in this high valley called Schams. The fields were very small, the soil extremely rocky. Here and there were stone fences. For the first time we began to see old wooden houses and barns, some of log, with stone roofs. This, too, felt *italienisch* (Annemarie pointed out painted names on buildings in Andeer written in Romansh) but of a much poorer sort than in the *Herrschaftsland* of Malans and Maienfeld. This was, had been, peasant country. We were within ten or twelve kilometers of Italy, due south, and twenty-five kilometers of Saint Bernard's Pass, to the southwest, famous for its puppies as big as ponies.

In Andeer we had coffee and tea in an upscale coffee shop and then headed back through Zillis to Thusis. This time Annemarie took the new highway, with lots of very modern tunnels, that more or less parallels the Viamala. We scooted right on through Thusis to Bonaduz and Chur.

In Chur, in the deepening darkness, Annemarie took us (she wasn't done with us yet) to supper at *Gasthaus Stern* (Hotel Star). Once again we were in a dining room a century old, with wonderful wooden walls, ceiling, tables, and chairs; but this was more sedate and a lot less eccentric than Castels. We were waited on by a buxom young woman from East Germany who was attentive, efficient, and a little stern—I mean no pun on the name of the hotel—maybe I should say grim. The food was good. Susanna and Annemarie ordered *Maluns*, pronounced "ma-loons," a dish of cooked potatoes, grated, mixed with flour and fried, served with Alp cheese and warm apple sauce. I had an *Engadiner Wurst*, a sausage from the Engadine valley along the Inn River, and what amounted to hashbrown potatoes, and *Veltliner* wine.

From Chur we drove directly and quickly north along the Rhine to Buchs. Off to the east, the "jewels" of Liechtenstein were pinpoints of light webbing the stone mountain: *Liechtenstein*, indeed! We found the *Bahnhof* and waited for the *Postauto*, the bus. When the bus arrived, Annemarie came in with us. We thanked her to the limits of her tolerance. She left—we waved and waved—the bus took off. We went to Grabs, to Gams, through Wildhaus and Unterwasser and Alt St. Johann, and got off at Stein, at ten o'clock, and walked, happy and tired and puffing, up the "snow-covered and slippery" narrow, winding road to the Juons' "weekend house"—though Susanna only says "weekend house" when she talks of it in English. Its real High German name is *das Kühhaus*, and its Swiss dialect name is *s' Chüehuus*—both of which mean "cow house," and is known as such by local people and on local maps. The sky was moonless but full of stars: there, for the first time since coming to Switzerland, I saw my old friend the Big Dipper, pointing with complete faithfulness to the *Nord Stern*, the same as she does over our little log house in the woods of northern Wisconsin.

Irma met us at the—yes—old, wide, and short wooden door, ushered us in with a hushed voice (everyone else was in bed), showed us to the attic, and wished us *Gute Nacht*. We crawled in, huddled up, and slept close and cold, happy as clams, fine as frogs' hair, *almost* as snug as two bugs in a rug.

If Susanna has a *home* in Switzerland, this is it.

Monday morning
February 19

Vater, *mit der Zigarre*, comes into the music room, walks around the shiny black grand piano, bends to peer through the window at the thermometer fastened to the exterior window frame, and walks back to the door. A little startled, he notices me sitting on the far end of the couch, near the shut-tered fireplace—startled, I think, because I rarely sit here to write. Briefly he comes to sit beside me, smiles, and says something positive (I am ashamed how little *Schweizerdeutsch* I've picked up) about my *Kompendium*. I smile in return, he leaves, and I go to check the temperature: 3° C.

I thought Wisconsin the prima donna of fickle weather, but the previous few days have caused me to reconsider. Right now it's snowing, very lightly, and the ground has a thin white blanket.

Well, I'll start at the other end of this narrative.

The author at work on his Kompendium.

Friday morning, at the cow house, it was cloudy. After breakfast, in the small kitchen with the very low ceiling, I sat and wrote at the walnut table. All the young people—Rosemarie and her friend Estelle, Barbara, and Simon—went skiing. Susanna wanted to show me something of the valley called Laad, to the west; so she, Irma, Hanspeter, and I set out walking, three of us pulling sturdy wooden sleds with wooden runners edged with metal.

I thought we would be going up the road until it ended. We walked past small farms and old farmhouses, past an old sawmill perched right on the bank of the *Weissthur*, the White Thur. (Later I was told this sawmill used to, and maybe still does, operate by water power.) We crossed the *Weissthur*—a little river with very clear water, snow muffins on all rocks above waterline—and, to my surprise,

The Weissthur.

after another half hour, ended up in *Gasthaus Speer* (Hotel Arrow), which is perched on a hillside not more than a quarter-mile from the cow house, but separated from it by the deep valley through which the White Thur tumbles.

Gasthaus Speer is a big, sprawling three-and-a-half story ramshackle inn which combines the functions of local tavern (there was a juke box and, on the wall, the house rules for the national card game, *Jass*), a restaurant (we had some delicious freshly-made deep-fried filled pastries called *Zigerchröpfli*), a hotel, and

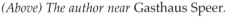
(*Above*) *The author near* Gasthaus Speer.

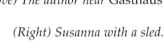
(*Right*) *Susanna with a sled.*

probably living quarters.

Hanspeter, Irma, and Susanna rode sleds down the curving road most of the way to the bridge. When I caught up with them, we walked back to the cow house, the mountain tops lost in clouds.

That evening, just before supper, Estelle joined me in the low, wooden, warm living room with the dark green tile stove. (I am slightly over six feet tall. There are several rooms in the cow house in which I cannot stand straight. I learned very quickly to walk slightly stooped, with bent knees.) To my surprise (she had been silent at breakfast) Estelle began speaking English. She explained she has spoken French from childhood—her mother was born in France; that she had to learn German in school; that she was taught English for three months in a school in England and then became a governess for a family in London for six months. Estelle was thin, shy, and introverted. In some ways she quickly reminded me of my daughter, Hannah, who is a Peace Corps volunteer in Ivory Coast, in Africa, and who also speaks French. And so I immediately warmed to Estelle—partly, I suppose, for her English, but not entirely so. There was also some protective, fatherly impulse at work, for Irma's and Hanspeter's children are loud, extroverted, argumentative, beaming, and witty—like a flock of restless parrots surrounding a quiet canary. So for a little while this old crow took a shy canary under his wing.

Friday night a hard wind began to blow. Sometime in the middle of the night it woke us. The wind moaned, the house creaked and groaned, a shutter began banging and slamming. Susanna got up, opened our only bedroom windows, pulled both shutters closed and latched them. It was hard to tell when morning came because of the darkness in our frosty bedroom.

On Saturday there was snow, serious snow, heavy snow. The kids were restless and grumpy because it made for poor skiing. Pretty soon Hanspeter took Rosemarie and Estelle to Nesslau to catch a train: they were returning to Lucerne. Before they left, Susanna and I gave Estelle our address and urged her to come stay with us, if ever she travels to America; Quebec, with its quaint French, is definitely on her list of attractions. In the early afternoon, all the rest of us except Simon drove down to Stein. Here Susanna and I said goodbye to Irma, who was on her way—Hanspeter and Barbara were taking her to the train in Nesslau—to Germany, via Lucerne, to hear Julia sing in an opera.

Susanna showed me around Stein. We went, for instance, into the Protestant church. It was, in size and proportion, rather like the church in Zillis, but utterly lacking in solid peasant groundedness. It was nice. It was neat. It was rather boring.

And then we walked back up to the cow house in a virtual blizzard. The trees on the mountains were moaning in the wind. Grainy snow whipped our faces. It was wonderful. Simon met us on the road near the ski lift. He had quit, he said, because the wind was too awful.

That evening Hanspeter made supper—*Polenta*, essentially a cornmeal mush served with meatballs and a tomato sauce. We were a smaller crew eating heartily around the table: Hanspeter, Simon, Barbara, Susanna, myself, and a nine year-old girl from the farm just down the hill a little. (Susanna and I had gone to the farm, and into the barn, the previous evening, along with Simon, who was there to purchase milk and homemade butter. We came in just at milking time. The cows—all thirteen of them, and all Brown Swiss—were clean and in their stanchions.) This pudgy-faced girl with the brown ponytail and mouth that turned down in a natural frown was of course named Heidi—this is true—and when she smiled, which wasn't often, her whole face lit up. She most certainly was not afraid—maybe even a little indignant that anyone would think otherwise—to walk home alone in the dark.

On Sunday morning before we left (Simon went off to the ski lift), I asked Susanna to take me on a last tour of the building.

In typical style, the barn and house are one continuous construction. The only animal I saw in the barn was a reclusive grey and white cat. The whole long building (though various things in both house and barn have been added on, remodeled, and replaced) is about two hundred years old. Beethoven was a young man when the cow house was built. France was in the throes of its Revolution. George Washington was the president of the fledgling United States of America. The ceilings, as I've said, are almost all too low for a person six feet tall to stand erect. The floors, walls, ceilings, and doors are mostly unpainted lumber, some boards of which approach

Susanna in front of the cow house.

two feet in width. The upstairs floor is tongue-and-groove plank: and all the floors have that wonderful uneven sheen that comes with having been walked on for years and years and years. Every doorway is low and has a sill, as much as a foot high. The doors are fat and squat, some a little beat up, many with handmade hinges. There are virtually no closets, only wardrobes, many of these well over a century old with elaborately painted doors and big keys. In all, there are four bedrooms and two living rooms. The biggest of these living rooms was also the newest, and unheated. It was to the north side of the main part of the house and had been the "loom room" in the second half of the nineteenth century, when many farm families had supplemented their income by weaving.

I had this uneasy feeling, after our walk on Friday, that many of the small farms in this valley may well become "weekend houses" once farm commodity prices are pushed low enough by the European Union, G.A.T.T., and all the other "free trade" machinations of multi-national corporations and their compliant nation-states. The World Trade Organization, with its offices in Geneva!

Also, we had to scoot. Barbara gave Susanna and me little hand-woven bracelets she'd just made. I tucked under Simon's pillow a belt of mine he had very much admired. Down through Stein (Barbara grabbed a sled and beat us there) in Hanspeter's Toyota van—tire chains on the rear wheels—and on to Nesslau where the train ends (or begins, depending on how one looks at it—when you get to Nesslau will you be arriving or departing?) and where the "wild man" of the Toggenburg is buried: this hairy, naked man who was captured by mountain farmers in the late nineteenth century, who lived the remainder of his (reluctantly clothed) life in the Nesslau poorhouse, and who never spoke.

Here the sun was shining and we stood in the clean sunshine for maybe twenty minutes, waiting for the train, gawking at mountains as their thinking caps drifted away, chatting with Hanspeter and Barbara. We shook hands, we hugged, we kissed, we waved and waved. The train moved and twenty minutes later we hustled to change trains in Wattwil. At Lichtensteig, still wonderfully sunny, I caught a glimpse of the old city just before our clear path was swallowed by a tunnel. And I am learning to tell immediately upon entering a tunnel whether it is long or short by how much my eardrums hurt. They hurt a lot; the tunnel was long.

When we came out at Brunnadern, the sky was cloudy. Here the train went north, high above a lovely valley through which the Necker River flowed, a very homey-feeling place for some inexplicable reason. At Mogelsberg we went east, more or less, through Degersheim to Herisau. From this vantage point we could see, to the northeast, all the way across the Bodensee to Germany.

Here again I was struck less by the view itself (which was nevertheless imposing) than by the incredible magnitude of change in landscape and geography in such short distances that characterizes Switzerland. We had left Nesslau at 12:10 p.m., and we arrived in St. Gallen before one, with a fast train change in Wattwil. When God made Europe, He must have had one hand in the Mediterranean, the other in the North Sea, and squeezed—hard! What was to become Switzerland popped up over the top of Italy in an absolute jumble of valleys and mountain ranges, glaciers and fast-flowing rivers, forests and alpine meadows. One can easily imagine how He yodeled in surprise and satisfaction.

The day was a long way from being over. First stop in St. Gallen was the concrete passageway under the train tracks where a man wearing fingerless gloves was playing a classical guitar and singing. A sign by his feet said he was a student from Israel and needed money to get home. We added modestly to the collection of coins already there. He sang in a peculiar grating voice, but not unpleasantly so.

Next we went through the old city, frequently admiring and laughing at the costumes of people dressed up for *Fasnacht* (the Swiss equivalent of Mardi Gras), mostly kids. We saw little Indians, cowboys, spacemen, Snow White, animals of all sorts. There were large, noisy bands in vaguely look-a-like costumes, bands with lots of drums and wind instruments. From a distance, the clatter sounded like all the half-time bands in the world assembled for the goofiest football game ever played—the Newood Woodticks versus the Putz Alpinehorns—with no rules, no uniforms, no playing field, and

The Max Oertli sculpture.

several hundred players with bags stuffed with confetti and presumed irresponsible.

We were on our way to a two o'clock appointment with Susanna's godmother, Fridy Pietrogiovanna, and her husband, Paul. This took us down Museumstrasse, the street on which Susanna used to live. Walking near the museum we could barely see a sculpture Susanna was telling me about, a clownish man in bronze whose fingertips spurt water in the summer, made by the sculptor Max Oertli who was a friend of the Juons, in Susanna's childhood. We detoured to see it; and then, on impulse, went into the museum to see whether any Segantini cards might be for sale and whether any Segantini originals might be on display. The answer to both questions was Yes; but when the open-faced, grey-haired woman behind the front desk saw Susanna's hesitation at the Fr.6.00 per person entrance fee, she asked whether that might be too much for us. Susanna then explained (all this went on in *Schweizerdeutsch*) that we were from America and that we are invariably startled by the prices, that things are so much more expensive now than when she was a child and used to live nearby. The woman had been watching Susanna closely the entire time. Finally, she slowly reached across the counter, took

Susanna's hand and said softly, "Susanna, you look just like your mother!"

Wahnsinnig! Wunderbar! This woman, her husband (who was also Susanna's history teacher), and their two daughters, lived in the apartment directly below the Juons. After a hurried conversation, we were ushered into the Segantini gallery—ten marvelous original paintings—for free; and when we'd selected five Segantini cards, Frau Caderas insisted they too were free. We left amazed and bewildered: how do we come to be the recipients of such an endless shower of gifts?

Then we had to hurry past two hospitals, around a few corners, to get to Tante Fridy's apartment building. Before we'd even crossed her street we were "Yoo-hooed" from an open window on the fourth floor, with much waving of arms. We huffed and puffed our way up the stairwell—"only" fifty-seven steps, Tante Fridy said when she and Paul walked us down, later. (She is seventy-seven. He is a mere eighty-two.)

Tante Fridy was short and trim with a friendly face and unruly grey hair. Paul was tall and rather formal with a long face and neatly-combed grey-black hair. Both wore glasses. We were ushered with great ceremony into the living room. Cups and saucers for four, and a cake, were set out on a coffee table. After a little preliminary conversation, tea was served, and two kinds of cookies brought out. (I was sugared to my tonsils by the time we left.)

Tante Fridy spoke a little English. Paul spoke none. Most of the conversation was of old times—Tante Fridy was in Vater's Bach choir from beginning to end, all forty-one years of it—of family, of Mama and Vater and how they're doing. Virtually all of this (I noticed out the window that snow had begun to fall) went on in *Schweizerdeutsch* and, despite my best efforts, I began to fade. My eyelids grew heavy and my posture became slouchy. But then, somehow, the conversation turned to the European Union—ah, yes, Paul had worked for many years in a textile factory—and Susanna began translating and I perked up.

The gist of what they said was this: Switzerland has grown soft, hard times are coming, somewhere down the road there will be an economic collapse. Through Susanna I said this is exactly what my father, a retired farmer, has been saying for years.

And in my own mind I thought: Even with allowances for the grumps of old age, over the passing of the familiar, with every generation's faulty assumption that *my* childhood is normative and ideal, I nevertheless believe them. Great suffering lies ahead, especially for that part of the world, those classes, who imagine suffering has been "conquered."

Soon it was time, and a little past time, to hurry. On with coats and down the stairs—all fifty-seven of them—with Tante Fridy and Paul right behind us. They stood in the doorway and waved, both of them, big arm-swinging waves, until we were literally around the corner at the end of the street. Then we did really hurry with our bags and bundles, our old-fashioned coats and clompy boots—our everyday *wahnsinnig Fasnacht* garb—through the snow and slush, just in time once again to catch the train to Sulgen. Snow was falling. By the time the train stopped at Bischofszell, there was rain. At Sulgen, the snow had been largely washed away. We dashed to the *Altersheim* to see Mama. Vater was there, too. We chatted, we left. Vater drove us home in the gloomy dusk, in the rain.

At supper, Susanna told Vater the story of our travels and adventures. I listened half-asleep, washed dishes, took a bath, and went early, happily, contentedly to bed. And no *Alptraum* disturbed my slumber. And no banging shutters.

Monday night

It was snowing this morning when Susanna went in with Vater to see Mama, and it was sunny when she walked home, shortly past noon. As we prepared lunch, the Säntis was visible out the south kitchen window. I fixed us fried potatoes, fried onions, and an egg each.

The big news of the day is that Susanna and Vater have talked, Susanna and Mama have talked, Mama and Vater have talked—and, for the foreseeable future, Mama will stay in the *Altersheim*. Almost everybody we've talked to has been against Mama coming home: partly her condition, partly Vater's condition, and partly the general sense of helplessness in finding anyone who could, who would, take adequate care of Mama at home—essentially an "on call" twenty-four-hour-a-day job while cooking the meals, washing the clothes, and dealing with an anxious, hovering Vater.

This is a sweet-sour pill to swallow, a bowing to the apparent inevitable. Mama seems to have anticipated as much. Vater is guiltily relieved. And we—?

Wednesday morning
February 21

The sweet, melancholy sounds of Johann Sebastian Bach float up to me from Vater's grand piano, two floors down. Susanna's just on her way downstairs to put on her heavy coat and heavy shoes, and then see Mama. Will she walk to Sulgen this cloudy morning or will Vater drive her in the car? I don't know; but the music has stopped.

It's somehow hard to believe—and yet I deeply feel—that tomorrow we fly back to America. There is so much I will miss, even this little wooden room with the hard mattresses on the floor, and the portrait, painted in 1944 by Albert Schenker, of Vater and Mama, that hangs on the wall: Mama sitting with her hands clasped in her lap; Vater standing, just behind Mama's left shoulder, with a half-smoked *Zigarre* between the first two fingers of his right hand. They are both so young. Mama has tousled blond hair and rosy cheeks. Vater is tall and lean, with dark hair—but already with a receding hairline. They both look a little sad, somehow—one wonders whether there was some trouble in their lives—though maybe it was nothing more than the tedium of posing.

Mama gave up her career as gardener when she married Vater. The feeling persists in me that this was an enduring sadness and loss in her life, especially as they lived so many years in St. Gallen, in apartments with no garden space. Meanwhile, Vater was a very

The portrait of Mama and Vater.

successful music teacher, organist, and choir director: this morning, at breakfast, he said his career was virtually like a hobby, because it gave him such joy and pleasure.

This archetype—the woman who abandons her own pursuits so that her man might pursue his unimpeded—is rich in spiritual irony: the clergyman who preaches the high virtue of Christian servanthood, then goes home to the wife who serves him his dinner and washes his socks. But we must also beware of turning this archetype into a rigid mental mold into which we cast our impressions of real people. Nothing and nobody ever quite fits our preconceptions.

Yesterday, in Annemarie's apartment in St. Gallen, I asked if she ever considered going elsewhere—say to Africa—to practice medicine. She said she definitely had considered it, but destiny had never quite opened for her in that way. Then she went on to say that a surgeon with whom she had worked for many years had, as a young doctor, worked with Albert Schweitzer (who was French, not Swiss) in his hospital in Lambarene, Gabone; that he continued on in Gabone after Schweitzer's death in 1965; had come back to Switzerland to raise a family; and now, in retirement, was in charge of a floor in a halfway house in Zürich for drug addicts and AIDS patients.

Last evening, as we trudged up the long hill to the Buchenberg (we could see its light a half-mile away), Susanna said a little wall plaque in Annemarie's tiny, cluttered kitchen read: "That person is happiest who gives the greatest joy to the most people." Susanna and I can definitely be added to the list of those to whom Annemarie has given joy.

We had walked to Sulgen and were on the platform of the *Bahnhof* by eight o'clock in the morning. The usual cloudiness. Once on the train, I watched for the iron footbridge across the Thur, just upstream from Kradolf—the footbridge I will not get to walk across this visit, nor the footpaths, the *Wanderwege*, on the other side that follow the river upstream and down, through woods and along the edges of fields.

In the *Bahnhof* in St. Gallen, a fellow in yellow *Fasnacht* costume, dressed clownlike with a painted face, was playing a drum and dancing; but nobody was paying him much attention. We bought flowers for Frau Alice Luginbühl and for Annemarie, and we visited them in sequence.

Frau Luginbühl is the wife of the late professor who was Susanna's godfather. She is a slightly stooped, imposing lady with unkempt steel-grey hair and trembling hands, and who had ready for us open-faced sandwiches, tea, and a crumpled pastry called *Storchenäscht*, "stork nest." From eighteen months in England, with an uncle, over sixty years ago, Frau Luginbühl was able to converse with me in English quite well, thank you. She and her uncle had lived in the north of England, near Scotland, with much coal-burning industry, and she was forever washing soot off her hands.

Frau Luginbühl's apartment—surprisingly large for an old lady, with lots of books and a very nice parquet floor—is on the third floor of a building on the north slope of the valley that is St. Gallen. From her large (and very clean) windows that look south, we could see a great deal of the old city and across it to the south slope with fields and orchards and fence lines and farm buildings, all crowned with forest—the whole scene blanketed with clean snow. This was a Grandma Moses painting on an enormous scale. And it was somehow especially wonderful when considered against the age of this settlement, dating back for sure to the seventh century: what compactness, conservation, and attention to detail can accomplish.

Annemarie, too, was prepared for us—though I had to sit in the living room with a book about Graubünden while Susanna was taken to the kitchen to render a verdict on *which* salad was most appropriate. Plants had begun to take over the apartment—especially imposing was a *Christusdorn*, a Christ's-thorn, that sprawled from its home base in an antique Graubünden cradle, handmade, painted blue-grey with much artwork, and the date 1739 painted on one end. About the only object not threatened by jungle was the grand piano.

Ushered into the dining room, small and full of plants, we were served a wonderful yellow rice dish with mushrooms, very thin dried pink *Fleisch* from Graubünden, one of the green salads, a carbonated water, and a fine red wine. Later, back in the living room, we had several small cups of coffee, a compressed cake from Graubünden called *Bündner Nusstorte*, and sweet tangerines with very orange skins and lots of tiny seeds. Among her parting gifts for us was a booklet on St. Martin's church in Zillis and—from Walter Sutter—*An Outline History of Switzerland*, in English, by Dieter Fahrni.

Annemarie walked us part of the way down the hill. When we parted—we going further down, she going back up—we all would stop and turn and wave, go on for a little way, and do it all over again until we were out of sight. Saint Annemarie....

We made the 4:05 *Zug* in plenty of time—that is to say, we could begin to breathe before it left—and we were well over an hour with Mama in the *Altersheim* (in fact, I fell asleep on her bed) before we walked home in the dark.

Mama. I wish I could say more about Mama—for she was the essential tug that brought us here, and yet I've said the least about her. In her presence I've been largely quiet. To some extent, this has been deference to Susanna and Vater. To some extent, it has been the language barrier compounded by deference to Susanna and Vater. And to some extent, and more with Mama than with anyone else I've been able to communicate with, I've been reluctant to probe, to ask leading questions—partly because I suspect painfulness in her life's sacrifice, partly because I do not wish to disturb the equilibrium she seems to have achieved in her old age, in her relative feebleness.

I very much admire her occasional beaming smile, childlike almost and fully in the present, and her very dry humor, aimed largely at herself. And I continue to cringe when I feel her old bones move in my grasp.

Almost I wish we could stay another two or three weeks, to see the early flowers come. (Two days ago, Susanna picked the very first *Erantus*, a yellow flower like our marsh marigold, only smaller.)

The task is now to incorporate this wonderful Swiss experience into our woodsy life in the north of Wisconsin, with its quasi-European cultural rawness: we who pushed aside the Indians, expropriated their land, forced them onto reservations; we who have lived in a jumble of incessant change ever since, yesterday's pattern broken by today's invention; we who cannot distinguish cultural necessity from technological fascination; we who talk expansively about the wave of the future as the past lies in shambles at our feet.

But the flowers will bloom again this spring. Somewhere around the first of May, the marsh marigolds with their delicate yellow flowers and large, rounded, dark green leaves will literally blanket the creek banks beneath the alders. *Gell?*

May there always be wild flowers and untamed little creeks with trout in gurgling, cold water. May there always be bouquets for those we love. And may there always be someone to love.

Wednesday evening

Shortly after noon Susanna came home, bundled-up and rosy-cheeked. While she began to sort for packing, I fixed us a lunch of boiled potatoes, onions, *Wurst*, bread and butter. While cooking, I noticed out the east window, near the greenhouse and in the bushes, a little *Rotkehlchen*, that delicate brown bird with the faintly orange bib that will forever inappropriately be to me a "roadkill" because of that goofy moment in Irma's kitchen.

During lunch, Susanna talked of Mama and of her suppressed yearning to be home; but how she, Susanna, has to restrain her own impulse to give advice, to make suggestions, to intrude into this difficult and puzzling situation, compounded by thousands of earth miles and a vast ocean.

We ate. I looked out the south window, over the small green kitchen table, to the orange and red and brown tile roofs of Götighofen, the half-timbered and stucco farmhouses, the grey-white wood smoke drifting from chimneys—this little village of which I've become so fond.

At three, exactly, we went quickly, all three of us, to Frau Margrit Lässker's cozy little house, squeezed between this backyard and the vineyard that crowns the hill. With her usual irrepressible exuberance, Frau Lässker met us at her door and ushered us up the crooked staircase to her living room and dining room. This is the most cozy house I've been in, in Switzerland. We had to sit immediately at the table, and Margrit brought out a *Zwetschgen Kuchen*, a Graubünden plumcake, to which she added whipped cream and a sprinkling of sugar. And, of course, pearbread. Plus coffee.

The talk bubbled along in *Schweizerdeutsch*, and I was content to take a bubble bath in its sounds, not trying very hard to pick out the words I know, nibbling *Kuchen*, sipping coffee, and indulging in a mellow melancholy. I like Margrit—this small, strong woman in her late seventies who rises at five, eats a tiny breakfast, and plays the piano while the sun wakes the world. At four we left, with many warm and swaddling words of parting.

By four-thirty, we were on our way to the *Altersheim*. In many respects this was a typical visit with Mama: the joking (she said she'd gotten a job, just this afternoon, as a fog splitter), the tray of food brought in, the chatting with the nurse. But the leaving was hard— hugs and kisses and tears—a heavy joy, a grateful sorrow.

It was almost six when we passed the little pasture, in town, where sheep are kept. "It looks like they've eaten all the bread," Susanna said. She'd told me at lunch that someone had dumped a bag of dry bread over the fence, and that the sheep were eagerly eating. I thought of the little poem I'd written nearly twenty-five years ago, from some scrapes of conversation I'd overheard my young son Tobias having with his friend Paul David Steffen:

I would give milk
to sheep, one said,
and to cows I would
feed bread. It's easy
to catch a goat,
the other said,
chasing chickens
is a joke.
All the sunshine
makes a shadow;
all the shadows
make for rain.
Where do you suppose
the wool comes from?
And how about
the grain?

And then—

Well, first I have to say that on several occasions, while walking to and from Sulgen, we've seen tracks of *Rehe*, the local wild deer. I mentioned to Susanna several times how much I'd like to see one before we left. And several times she told me it would be about as likely as a tourist in northern Wisconsin seeing a wolf or a bear. In other words, forget it.

The road east out of Sulgen goes on to Romanshorn. But just out of town, a road branches off to the southeast, across the railroad tracks and then uphill toward Götighofen. There is a field, a pasture, on either side of this road, right across the tracks—and there, in the field on the right, in deep dusk, were seven deer, seven *Rehe*, smaller and more compact than our whitetails, with their heads up, alert, watching us drive by.

"I think this is your going-away present," said Susanna Maria Juon-Gilk, *Mutterland* of my heart.

late Sunday afternoon
February 25

Sunny and bright at the log house, in Newood, in Wisconsin, in the U.S.A. Not a cloud to be seen in the western sky, through the window with buzzing flies, as I sit on the bed upstairs, my back against the fieldstone chimney.

My father and our house-sitting friend Charlie Green were waiting for us at the Central Wisconsin Airport Thursday evening. We'd left Zürich around ten a.m. and arrived in Chicago, very tired and a little bewildered, shortly after one p.m. That made it (contrary to the numbers which make it, on the surface, seem short) a very long day. I was asleep almost instantly by nine p.m. but woke—and was wide awake—shortly after four a.m.

Friday we did putzy things, creaturely things, by which we convinced ourselves we really had come home.

Saturday morning, Susanna and I drove to Duluth, Minnesota, to get Woody (the bay by Ashland was frozen, but Lake Superior in its vast reaches was as blue as ever), and then back home by dark: just a little four-hundred mile car trip as a sort of homeopathic remedy for jet lag.

Everyone we've met, including our friends at church this morning, have had stories to tell of the cold we were so fortunate to miss. (My father's thermometer has numbers to fifty below zero, Fahrenheit. The thin red line disappeared into its vial, below the numbers. He therefore estimated the temperature at a negative fifty-five!) But it's been mild and melty since we've been back. The first birds to return in spring—horned larks—are already to be seen on the bare shoulders of the roads. Our long driveway through the woods is impassable but—hey!—Susanna's talking about gardens.

Thursday morning we were up early—a quick breakfast—and Annemarie came to take us to the *Bahnhof* in Sulgen. There was a light dusting of fresh snow.

I had tears in my eyes when we parted from Mama Wednesday

night—there she stood, her frail, stooped self, waving goodbye and calling *"tschau"* (pronounced "chow" and meaning goodbye) as the elevator door thumped shut. And I had tears again when I hugged Vater (his nightshirt showing at the neck of his sweater) at the big door of the Buchenberg Thursday morning.

We were actually early, for a change, at the *Bahnhof*. But when the *Zug* arrived in a flurry of snow from Romanshorn, we had to hustle with all our gear. Annemarie grabbed Susanna's violin and hurried to the far door of our coach. Susanna almost didn't reach her or the violin before the train took off. We hardly had time to wave goodbye.

The coach was rather crowded with students, most of whom eventually got off at Winterthur. Susanna and I had to sit on opposite sides of the aisle. Lazy flakes of snow were in the air at Weinfelden.

I gazed out the window at the Swiss countryside, in the blue-grey light of early morning, at the snow-covered fields, the carefully-pruned fruit trees, the pencil lines of trellised grapevines drawn in exact rows down the hillsides, church steeples and farmsteads with a fresh dusting of snow on tile roofs. Little groups of crows flapped over fields. And then, between Frauenfeld and Winterthur, loping across an open field between the rail bed and a distant farm, small but long and lean with a great bushy tail—a fox! *Wunderbar!*

All too soon we were underground at Kloten, in the *Bahnhof* basement of the *Flughafen*, and off the train. Our gear in a cart, we walked and rode escalators, reversing our route of January 12. (January 12! We only just got here!) In the place where the Bolivian panpipe player had been there was instead a harp player from Paraguay, Omar Vera, with whom we also traded a tape. Señor Vera was dressed in a black sarape with gold fringe, the black rainbowed with thin brilliant colors. South American music to welcome us to Switzerland, and also to send us on our way. *Wahnsinnig!*

We had the usual minor frustrations with security. Still a little snow in the air as we boarded the 767, and light snow yet as the "Elephant" came to deice the wings.

At 10:05 a.m., Swiss time, under terrific jet engine thrust, we took to the air and very quickly lost sight of the earth, except for fuzzy glimpses. High over France, for a while, we could see the miniature earth, rivers like silver wire, towns of scattered beads, forests of short dark fur. And then clouds without an opening until we were out over the Atlantic. Once, in a cloud gap, I saw a ship crawling like a rusty tomato worm on slightly rippled blue-green water, leaving a tiny streak of froth in its wake.

The amazing thing was how *slowly* the *Unterwelt*, the under-world, seemed to creep by. On a bicycle at this apparent rate of speed, one would topple for lack of adequate momentum. By mid-Atlantic, a mild (but also mildly alarming) case of claustrophobia began to blossom its wilty leaves within me. Partly I was becoming rather des-perate for some *fresh* air. I began to indulge in fantasies of the pilot being forced to land on the ocean, of drifting on a raft (I checked to see where my wool coat and journal were stashed), of being picked up by a freighter....The ocean went on for a *very* long time. There is, so to speak, a heap of water in this world.

Over southern Canada we could, for a while, see miniature wild landscape. And then there was an immense, unbroken cloud cover all the way to Chicago, into which we dropped and slid to a slightly jerky landing—the grateful disembarking, the long walk to customs, the luggage, the cart, the airport train to Terminal 3, and eventually the much shorter flight, over clouds rumpled like woolen batting from an old quilt, to CWA, Central Wisconsin Airport, the black stew-ardess with a Caribbean accent serving juice and soft drinks.

The pilot took us below the clouds many miles south of the air-port. And so we could see, in the dim, grey light, the Wisconsin coun-tryside slide away beneath us: the larger blocks of woods, the farms, the gridwork of roads, the dark patches of ginseng beds under slat-ted roofs. This countryside looked scruffier, more raw and surly, than the carefully pruned and tended Swiss countryside we had so recent-ly left.

There is an immense horizon of sunset, peach and pink, out the big west window. My nine year-old son has come up to lie beside me, and has fallen asleep. The sunset glows above the snow-covered fields my father cleared from brush and stumps and rocks, in his young manhood, fifty, sixty years ago. These fields, pink with sunset on snow, are no longer in the family: only one farm, a big one, left in the neighborhood, and its proprietors struggling with cancer.

Change comes too fast. We are tossed by its turbulence—divorce, drugs, children in trouble, crime. In the attention-grabbing attractions of technology, we do not grasp the significance of cultural stability and the importance of spiritual concentration. Our lives are constantly disrupted by novelty and whim.

So we have plunged—so said the late Swiss psychiatrist Carl Jung—down a "cataract of progress." We need, he said, a serious remedy of "reform by retrogression," a return to cultural stability, a less energy-intensive life—"backwards a little, you know what I mean?"

The light of day has faded. There is a high, bright, quarter-moon in the southern sky. I strike a match to light a kerosene lamp, to illuminate these final words. Downstairs, water heats, humming, on the wood-burning cookstove, and Susanna sings *"Seit ich Dich für mich sehe"* ("Since I have seen you for myself") by Hans Roelli, the Swiss Woody Guthrie. The sweet melody and words float up to me.

I arrive at your door in the blueness of the evening. In your heart I can rise like the moon and the stars.

In your heart I will rise like the stars and the moon. In your heart I will rise. I have seen you for myself.

Auf Wiedersehen, Guten Abend und Gute Nacht. Perhaps we will meet again rather soon. The world is an unpredictable miracle, wheeling through an eternity of space. Is it not so? *Gell?*

Postscript

Du meines Herzens Freude, Du meines Lebens Licht,
Du ziehst mich, wenn ich scheide, hin vor Dein Angesicht
ins Haus der ewgen Wonne, da ich stets freudenvoll
gleich als die helle Sonne mit andern leuchten soll.

—Paul Gerhardt, Author

You my heart's joy, you my life's light,
You draw me, when I part, there before your face
into the house of everlasting bliss, where I am always filled with joy
like the bright sun with others shall shine.

IRMA JUON-MÜLLER

Heute morgen früh, am 26. Juli 1996 hat sie uns im 85. Lebensjahr verlassen, um in eine nie zu erahnende Herrlichkeit einzugehen.

(Today, early in the morning of July 26, 1996, she left us in her 85th living year, that she might go to an unimaginable glory.)

In grosser Dankbarkeit:

Andreas Juon-Müller, Götighofen
Julia Juon und Hermann Feuchter, D-Kassel
Irma und Hans-Peter Schoch-Juon, Adligenswil
Susanna und Paul Gilk-Juon, Merrill, USA
Anverwandte und Freunde

Der Gedenkgottesdienst findet am Mittwoch, 31. Juli in der Kirche Sulgen statt. Besammlung auf dem Friedhof um 14.00 Uhr.

(The memorial service will be on Wednesday, July 31, in the church of Sulgen. Gathering at the cemetery at 2 p.m.)